ART MATERIALS

ARTISTS' MATERIALS

Which, Why and How

Emma Pearce

A & C Black · London

First published in Great Britain by
A & C Black (Publishers) Limited
35 Bedford Row, London, WC1R 4JH

ISBN 0–7136–3554–1

A CIP catalogue record for this book is available from the British Library.

Typeset in Lasercomp Berkeley and Walbaum by
August Filmsetting, Haydock, St Helens
Printed and bound in Great Britain by
The Bath Press Ltd, Avon

IMPORTANT

Many of the substances described in this book are highly toxic and/or inflammable. Please read the *Health and Safety* section (page 9) in the *Preface*.

Although health and safety warnings are given throughout this book wherever they seem appropriate, in relation to both raw materials and ways of using them, neither author nor publisher can be held responsible for any harm which may come to anyone as a result of contact with or use of artists' materials. The information given is based on details supplied by manufacturers, in health and safety books, and from experience.

CONTENTS

PREFACE

I have, in this book, tried to establish what is and what is not necessary in methods and materials in order, *a.* to offer the maximum creative opportunity to the artist, and *b.* for the work to have the slowest rate of change.

To satisfy these criteria, I have amalgamated all the information possible, using one word – *Why?*

This is the most important thing for the artist to know. Without knowing *why* a particular medium or method is used, you cannot invent a substitute. In each chapter I have tried to establish the set of *whys?* for a particular medium. Once that group is identified, I have suggested a twin group of *hows?*. There are also the *whys* for these *hows*!

I hope that once you can see these *whys* you will be able to trust this book, simplify your methods and produce more work within the given criteria. The criteria can also be used to some extent inversely, i.e. to obtain a fast rate of change when you want it.

Although the contents of this book are mostly relevant to painters, I believe it will also be a valuable source of information for all artists. If nothing else, I hope that artists may learn the art of asking, 'Why?'

Maximum creative opportunity cannot come just from the material itself, especially if you tackle an area like encaustic or tempera, where you have a different set of mechanics to deal with. You will only discover the diversity of opportunity by becoming involved and working hard. However, you must not allow 'technical matters' to interfere with your creativity. This comes with experience as you get used to new information and ways of working.

A medium which is new to you is likely to sound absurdly complicated, e.g. needing a heat source to move encaustic around on its support. In fact, oils too, appear absurdly complicated if you are not familiar with them. Use a medium only if its characteristics suit you at the time. There is no point in using tempera if watercolour will do, or oil if acrylic is suitable, etc.

Obviously there is an infinite number of ways to do things, e.g., there is more than one way to fold canvas over a stretcher corner. Provided you take note of the reasons *why* a method is suggested you can then use your own.

Some sections, like *Stretching paper* are quite long. This is because the procedure often fails due to a lack of simple information. The oil chapter is so long partly because the medium is so versatile; partly because it has been used so much; and partly because it contains sections like *Types of canvas* which are not used solely in oil painting.

Don't be afraid of preparing your own supports or materials, there's room for mistakes whilst you're learning. An effort at a sound method is bound to be better than using an inappropriate one. Competence is necessary but it will come with experience.

When preparing supports, don't prepare one at a time, it is almost as quick to do two and will also save money. The same applies for making chalk pastels, etc.

Alternative ingredients and information are given, often at the end of a chapter. This is partly to give you a more complete picture and partly to help you become involved and practised, as you will have to make decisions for yourself if you are going to reach the standard you want, e.g. with gesso boards, the standards and surfaces possible are infinite; or making chalk or wax pastels; or priming a new type of support.

When mixing media, if you can satisfy the requirements for each there will be no problem combining them.

The rates of change expected of artwork are very slow compared to other commercial expectations. Unless the rate of change is a deliberate constituent of your work, we should expect and require our work to be practically unchanged in our lifetime. Products in other walks of life are more readily expected to fail.

Any reference to prices are to those relevant in 1991. Both metric and UK imperial measurements are given. In some cases a mixture of the two is easiest, e.g. 40 g of rabbit-skin glue to 2 pints of water.

Comprehensive information on materials and methods could not always be provided without crossing over various sections of the book. Please check cross references and use the index to optimise your use of the information. Definitions of materials are all indexed.

Discussion of artists' materials, particularly paints and explanation of details in *Appendix A*

I would like to argue that the artist should be the decision maker with his/her own materials. However, paint cannot be produced without the manufacturer making decisions first.

Manufacturers may decide any of the following: to match each new batch of paint to a set standard for that colour; to add wax-like materials to stabilize awkward pigments; to standardize consistency; or to add inert pigments to some colours which are too strong to use on their own. Any of these decisions can be made by the manufacturer without decreasing the number of decisions which can be made by the artist, provided they do not go beyond a certain point. Sometimes, to achieve their own defined objectives, manufacturers do need to go beyond this point.

Introducing additional elements to the original pigment can reduce its colour strength and cause noticeable differences in the brightness of colour between two makes of paint. Nevertheless, an absence of moderating factors will allow characteristics of difficult pigments to dominate, leaving the artist to cope with them.

The brand details in *Appendix A* are provided to give artists an indication of what can make products handle differently, and to provide, as far as possible, a thorough, informative guide to lightfastness.

'To balance colour ranges' is used in the tables to indicate that inert pigment has been used to enhance the colour range rather than to save money by reducing the coloured pigment content, e.g. some colours, particularly synthetic organic ones, are so strong, they dominate the palette excessively unless they are extended.

As I have mentioned under *Hopes for future materials* (below), the information given cannot be as accurate as a manufacturer's yearly product catalogue could be. Details of products in *Appendix A* must be used as guides. For instance, different manufacturers may not agree on the difference between a stabilizer and an extender and so may have given me conflicting information on products which may be extremely similar. Equally some manufacturers may have been on the cautious side when translating their lightfast ratings to the Blue Wool Scale, whilst others may have been too generous to themselves.

The columns stating the proportion of the ranges which are 7 or 8 on the Blue Wool Scale may look very different if there were a universal standard for artists. I have presented the information in this way as it is the only way I know how to give artists more information on products. It also offers manufacturers and retailers a suggestion on the type of specific information artists require and which would only serve to confirm the quality of their products. Please read *Lightfastness* (page 128) in the pigment chapter for a full explanation of the Blue Wool Scale and the many variables making this subject so difficult to standardize.

'No ratings' within the tables simply means the company has not published anything about lightfastness. In some cases this can mean that the lightfastness of the products is poor; but it may simply mean they haven't published anything. It seems a shame that artists are therefore unable to identify the good from the bad.

Artists can combine the information in *Appendix A* with their experience, to identify the paint they prefer.

'Student' or 'studio' ranges are often produced using less expensive pigments which can be extended with inert pigment to keep the price down. This is indicated in the tables by 'to reduce the pigment content'. Such ranges are produced to fulfil an economic purpose, whilst artists' ranges provide wider manipulative properties and are likely to be more lightfast. Student ranges are easily identifiable by their price.

Hopes for future materials

It would be wonderful if all manufacturers could present the Colour Index Generic Names and constituents of their materials as well as companies like Winsor & Newton and Talens do in their catalogues. Some companies do publish the information in a less clear form whilst others do not publish anything at all. It would also help if more companies used the Colour Index Generic Names on their tubes. More information along the lines of that given in *Appendix A* would be appreciated as discussed above. If manufacturers each produced details of paint contents and their effects, artists could build up experience on the resultant handling properties and be able to choose the material they want more accurately. Any such information would be more precise and up to date than I can give.

More extensive use by manufacturers of extremely lightfast colours (with a more accurate and universal rating system used by all companies) for artists would also alleviate the need for further explanation and information on lightfast ratings in comparison to the Blue Wool Scale, with all the accompanying inaccuraces, as I have had to do in this book. Such a system for information, labelling and lightfastness has been devised by the American Society for Testing and Materials (ASTM). The adoption of this system by manufacturers would remove the confusion that abounds at present. See *Bibliography*, page 169.

It would also be wonderful to see more companies making encaustic paint, surfaced rag paper, pigmented papers, etc.

Final note

Although I have tried to get to the bottom of every aspect of the media covered in this book, I hope manufacturers and readers alike will forgive me if I have omitted any information or inadvertently included any incorrect information. If nothing else, what is in this book gives you the format for finding out what you want to know about something which is not! The following subjects are not addressed in this book but the bibliography refers you to other relevant sources of information: Making hardwood panels; gesso sottile; distemper/size painting; fresco painting; casein painting; silicone ester painting.

There are infinite arguments, concerning every aspect of paint; ingredients, manufacture and use, with which I have not involved the reader. Each complete technical argument for and against something is a book in itself. I have tried to fulfil my original criteria by telling *why* and *how* specific artists' materials are used, believing this will be of value to artists.

HEALTH AND SAFETY

In addition to the notes made within each chapter, this section must be regarded for your good health.

Toxicity of artists' materials

Artist Beware by Michael McCann, published by Watson Guptill, is recommended for full information on toxicity of materials.

Children

Particular care should be taken by pregnant women and on behalf of children in an artist's studio.

Don't use artists' paint on children's toys. Small children are very easily poisoned, e.g. by chewing toxic paint films. Materials which are suitable for use by children or for children's toys will be labelled 'non-toxic'.

Cleanliness

Don't lick your brushes. Would you lick your palette? Use your common sense and be clean. Do not use your bathroom or kitchen as a studio, including the sinks. Do not eat, drink, or smoke with paint-covered hands and keep your nails free of any residues.

Avoid skin contact with very toxic pigments, e.g. white lead paint can still be absorbed through your skin.

A barrier cream should be used habitually. Use a water-based one for oil-based work and an oil-based one for water-based work. Do tell the supplier exactly what you need it for in order to get the most suitable one. See *List of sources*, page 165.

If painting with your hands regularly, surgical-type gloves would be the best protection and the least inhibiting. See *List of sources*, page 165.

Wear rubber gloves when you are cleaning up. See *Appendix B* (page 158) for methods of cleaning brushes and utensils.

Thinners

Turpentine and white spirit are both toxic, particularly by inhalation. Both are absorbed through the skin.

Don't use white spirit or turpentine to remove paint from your hands or skin. Not only can this cause skin problems but worse still, these thinners dilute paint and exacerbate the absorption of toxic pigments through the skin. What warm water and soap won't remove, a hand cleanser will. The safest ones are not based on petroleum. Make sure you ask the supplier for a non-petroleum-(solvent) based one. See *List of sources*, page 165.

Methylated spirits (industrial and mineralized) can be absorbed through the skin and is toxic by inhalation.

All three of these solvents can be fatal if ingested. Wear gloves when using them and never have a drink next to a jar of thinners, you might drink the wrong one!

Always work in a well ventilated area. You should not feel heady from the vapours.

Fixatives

Several fixatives use very toxic solvents. Use them outside.

Spraying fixatives, varnishes and paints

Sustained use of a spray gun or atomizer is not safe without protecting your skin and eyes and preventing inhalation of the spray. A safety equipment company will advise you on the correct safety apparatus.

Pigments

Dry pigments are probably the most toxic material you will handle. See pigment chapter, page 129.

Respirators

Respirators must be worn when handling toxic pigments. A safety equipment company will advise you on the correct fit and filter, but do tell them specifically what you need to be protected from. The filters must be changed regularly, ask the company to tell you how often. Contain the pigment dust as much as possible, i.e. don't spread pigment dust all over the room so you can breath it in when you take your respirator off. A cloth mask is not adequate to protect you from toxic pigments.

Chapter 1
OIL PAINTING

Oil paint can be used thinly or thickly, smooth or textured, opaque or transparent, used wet into wet, or wet on to dry. Once dry it is insoluble. Painting can be resumed at any time, but the original cannot be removed and pentimento should be considered (see page 37).

SUPPORTS

Canvas on open stretchers gives a sensitive receptive woven support on which to paint and provides a tooth for the primer and paint to grip.

Boards can be used if a hard weaveless surface is preferred. See gesso chapter (page 85) for types of board and their initial construction and preparation.

Canvas mounted on board can be used for a hard surface whilst retaining the texture of cloth.

Paper: Oil paint can acceptably be applied to a gelatin surface-sized, heavyweight rag paper (although it will be fragile) provided it is kept flat and supported in a portfolio or frame. Stretch the paper first and then size it once as for canvas. Any excessive use of medium or thinners is not recommended as they would soak into the paper. See paper (page 104) and watercolour (page 74) chapters and *Appendix C* (page 160). Millboard (a dense grey/brown paper-based board) can be used instead of hardboard and should be prepared in the same way as untempered hardboard (see page 89).

Other supports include, aluminium, steel, copper, glass, glass fibre, leather, parchment, vellum, marble, slate, ivory.

See *Supports (other)* in Bibliography (page 171) for sources of further information about preparation.

CANVAS

Canvas provides a surface which the priming and painting can grip. The less hygroscopic the canvas is, the less it will expand and contract and the better for long term tension. Artists' canvas, as opposed to other fabrics should be used because the thread has been evenly spun and woven, resulting in more even tension during the preparation of the canvas and the life of the painting.

Types of canvas

The various types of canvas each provide a different surface.

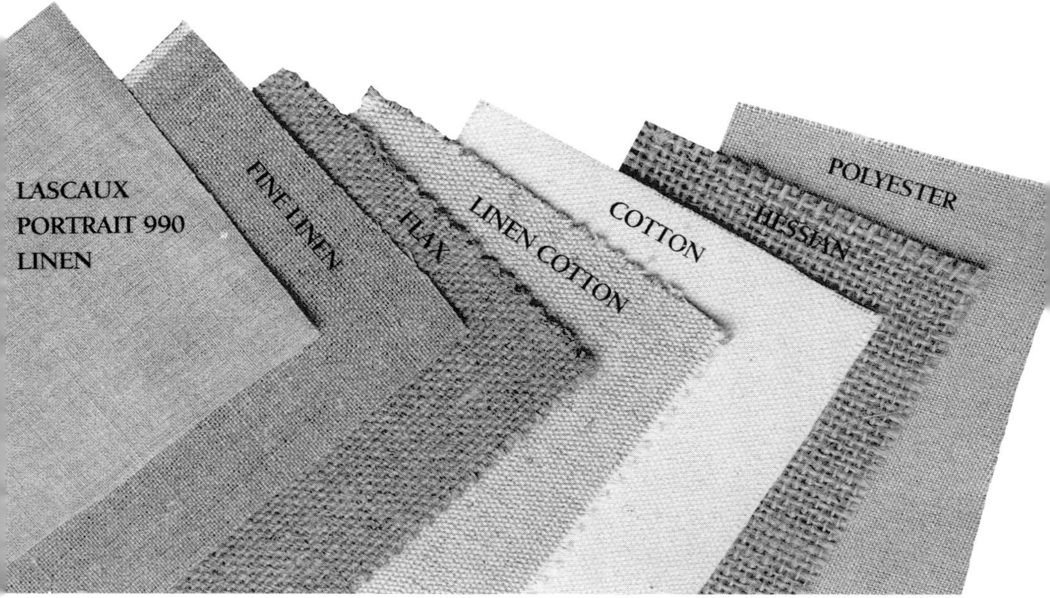

1. *Types of canvas.*

Pure unbleached linen is made from the flax plant from which linseed oil also comes. The heavier weave linen is often called flax canvas. It sizes, stretches and primes well and comes in three basic surface textures.

Bleached linen is not usually available and does not take sizing and priming as well as unbleached linen.

Cotton canvas (often called duck) does not size or prime structurally as well as linen. The size and primer tend to lie on the surface rather than grip the cloth. It does not have the physical property of stretching like linen. It comes in one basic surface texture, depending on the brand and has a less sensitive feel to it. It is approximately half the price of medium weight linen and 340 g (12 oz) cotton canvas is about equal in price to 340 g (12 oz) flax canvas.

Linen and cotton mixtures are not desirable to use for painting, despite the fact that the size and primer grip more than on cotton. The conflicting fibre characteristics create differing tensions across the cloth which outweigh any other advantages.

Natural and synthetic mixtures are not recommended for the same reason.

Hessian: Hemp and Jute do not take a ground at all well and quickly become brittle. They are very cheap. Flax canvas offers a similar surface to work on.

Polyester cloths are far less hygroscopic than a natural cloth, do not embrittle and hence suggest greater stability. They can come with different surface textures. Unfortunately, not enough research has yet been done on how to size and prime them for oil painting and those concerned with permanence should stick with linen or cotton.

Commercially prepared canvases and boards: There is no doubt that preparing your own supports will give you better control over your work. Primed canvas sold on a roll is difficult to stretch; an expandable stretcher is a must to get the canvas flat. The priming can also tend to be brittle.

Commercially prepared supports tend to look rather mechanical compared to ones prepared by the artist.

Initial preparation of canvas

A new piece of canvas resists the size, possibly from the use of starch by the manufacturer. It is important that the size goes into the cloth and doesn't float on top of it (see page 18). New cloth also shrinks when the size is applied. This produces an unnecessary tension in the cloth. Most warped canvases are due to this tension in the cloth putting the stretcher under undue stress. Both problems can be solved by rinsing the new cloth in water and drying it prior to putting it on the stretcher.

If you are cutting linen to fit a stretcher then measure the new cloth 25 cm (10″) longer in each direction than the dimensions of the stretcher to allow for shrinkage. A 50 × 75 cm (20 × 30″) stretcher needs a new piece of cloth 75 × 100 cm (30 × 39″). This includes enough overlap of canvas to fold over the stretcher bars as well. This is an average in case you don't know in which direction the width/length of the cloth is going. In fact a new piece of linen 184 cm (72″) in width will shrink to approximately 180 cm ($70\frac{1}{2}$″); whilst 184 cm (72″) from the length of the roll will shrink to approximately 171 cm (67″). Cotton shrinks far less than this and still resists the size.

Keep the creases to a minimum when wetting the cloth as they will not come out if you have squeezed it. They can interfere visually with your painting. To avoid creasing, wet manageable-sized pieces, lightly rolled, in as large a bath/sink as possible. Simply submerge the cloth until fully wet and then hang it up to drip dry. When damp-dry the cloth can be ironed on the hottest setting.

See *Using creased cloth* (page 17) if you must use creased canvas and for alternative methods of preparing the cloth (see page 17).

De-acidifying canvas

Before ironing you can de-acidify the canvas. This will at least double its life. However, canvases do last 300 years anyway! Canvas can also be de-acidified for use with acrylics etc.

This can be done by spraying it with a solution of fresh calcium hydroxide and water. See *List of sources* (page 165). Proprietary de-acidifying products are more expensive. Put 2 g of calcium hydroxide and a litre of distilled water in a bottle and shake it. Allow it to settle. Use the clear liquid in an atomizer (fig. 100) or garden spray (fig. 108) to spray the canvas. Leave to dry and then iron.

Sewing canvas together

Canvas can be joined together by sewing but the join will show. The thread should be the same fibre as the canvas and a strong sewing machine will be needed. Use a flat seam and keep the weave of the cloth running parallel up the join.

Stretching canvas

An adjustable stretcher makes it easier to get a flat canvas to the tension you want. See *List of sources* (page 165).

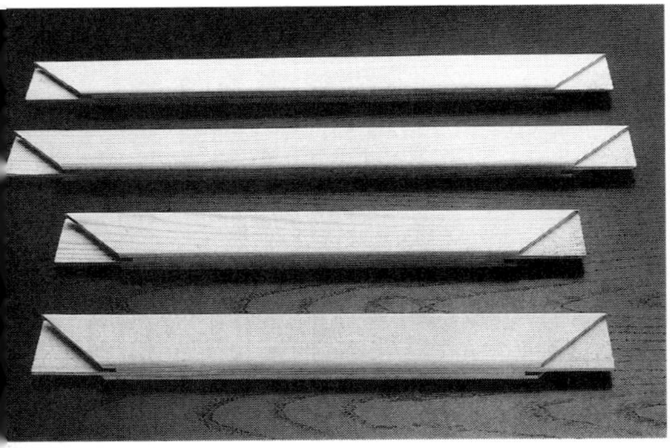

2. *Stretcher pieces.*

3. *Assembled stretcher.*

Making up a stretcher

For work under about 60 × 60 cm (24 × 24″), 45 mm ($1\frac{3}{4}$″) stretcher pieces can be used. For larger work use 57 mm and 70 mm ($2\frac{1}{4}$″ and $2\frac{3}{4}$″) pieces. A crossbar should be used for sizes over 71 cm × 91 cm (28 × 36″). Multiple crossbars should be used for larger works. Without them the stretchers are very flimsy.

Use a wooden mallet to put the stretcher pieces together. Drive the corners together until they meet. This leaves maximum room for expanding stretchers later.

N.B.: If there are any bevels make sure they all face one way. If there are crossbars, ensure the joint with the frame is below and not above the front surface of the frame, i.e. the crossbars are supposed to fit one way round.

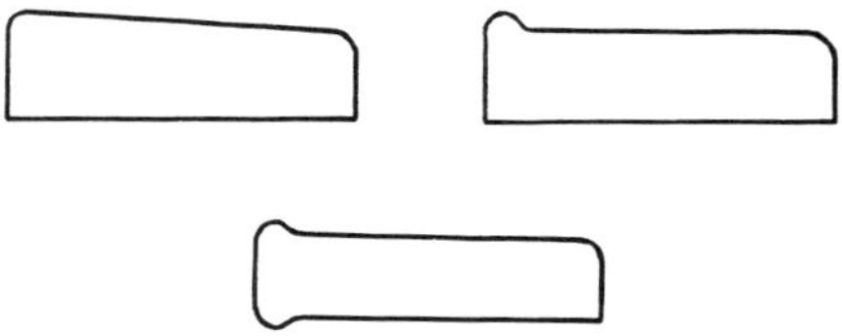

4. *Cross-sections of stretcher pieces showing variety of bevels.*

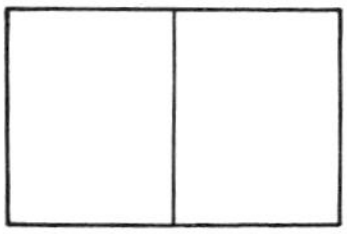

5a. *Chassis with one crossbar.*

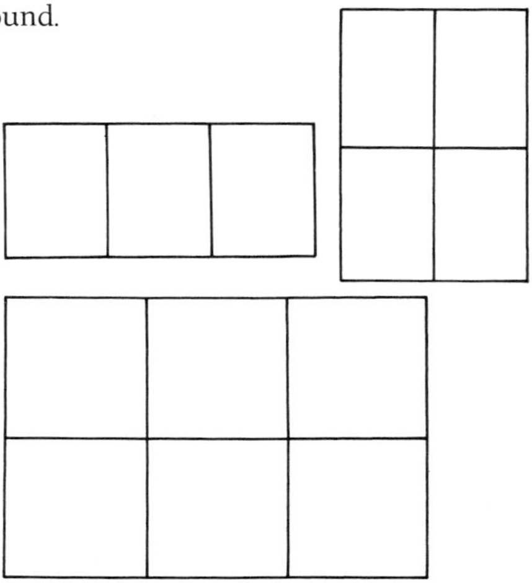

5b. *Three chassis with various multiple crossbars.*

The bevel prevents the inner edge showing as a ridge on the front of the canvas. See *Other stretcher designs*, page 18. A mason's set square can be used to ensure the chassis is square. Lie the chassis flat and butt up the square to each corner.

Keep working round the chassis until all the corners are square. You will find it easier to make small adjustments with your hands rather than the mallet. Once square, you can pin the tongue and groove joints together with four 12 mm ($\frac{1}{2}''$) tacks to prevent it being knocked out of true. These can be removed later if you use the wedges (USA: keys). The sized canvas will help to keep the chassis square once dry. See *Appendix B* (page 158) for photograph of other possible squares to use.

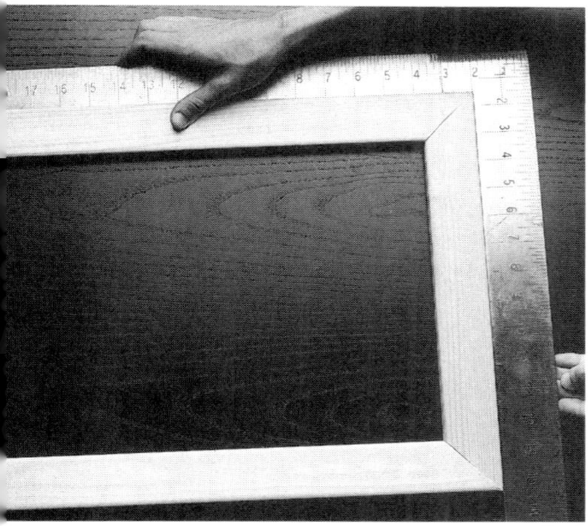

6. *Mason's square and chassis.*

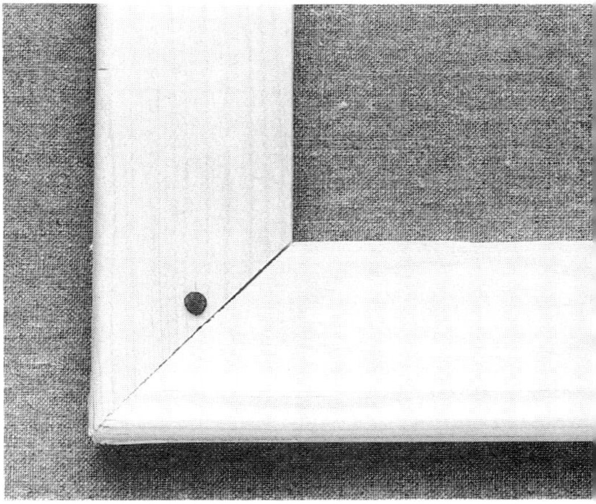

7. *Stretcher bar parallel with weave, and tack pinning together tongue and groove joint.*

Placing canvas on stretcher

Place the canvas on a flat surface and put the chassis bevel-side down with equal overlap all round. In order to be visually non-interfering and to promote equal tension, the weave of the cloth should run parallel with the stretcher bars. Unevenly pulled canvas will make the weave wavy on the front of the canvas.

Size contracts the canvas as the size dries. Linen stretches more successfully than cotton and therefore needs minimum pulling over the stretcher and can in fact be quite floppy. If you pull it too much the weave will not remain parallel with the stretcher. Cotton canvas does not stretch and therefore needs to be pulled tight and flat on to the stretcher. Canvas pliers will help with cotton, particularly on large canvases. In either case follow the weave of the cloth in relation to the stretcher bar as you attach the canvas.

Put the staples or tacks into the back of the chassis. Using the edge is awkward, makes framing difficult and reduces the durability of the canvas. Use 10 mm ($\frac{3}{8}''$) staples or tacks. Use heavy duty staples as lightweight ones rust too quickly. See *List of sources* (page 165) for staple guns. Put the first staple in the centre of one side and go

8. *Canvas stretched except corners.*

from the centre to one corner and then from the centre to the other corner. Do the same thing on the opposite side followed by the next two sides.

Corners

With the reverse of the chassis towards you, tuck the excess canvas on the top of the right-hand corner. Drive a staple into the back of this edge, this is the thickest part of the stretcher piece. Do this to all four right-hand ends.

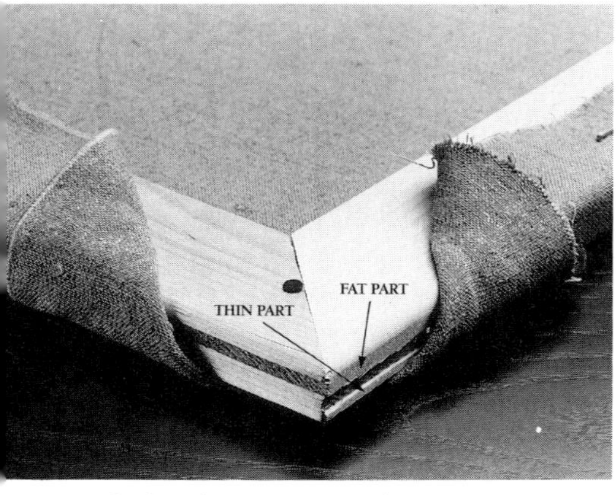

9. *Stretcher piece corner showing tongue and groove joint.*

10. *Final stretched corner pattern.*

Then go to each left-hand end and drive a staple into the front part of the stretcher edge (again the thickest part). This pattern avoids pinning the tongue and groved joint together with staples. Any loose canvas on the reverse of the stretcher can either be tacked together with a few stitches or will be covered by the paper backing (see page 29). Staples can be driven fully home by using a pin hammer.

11. *Stretched cotton* (left) *and linen.*

Using creased cloth

If you have to use a creased piece of cloth then either use a steam iron or use water in a garden spray to wet it as you iron. If the creases remain, the following procedure will reduce them further:

Stretch the canvas as normal.

Wedge the canvas out until there is approximately 1 mm gap in each stretcher joint.

Wet the canvas with water, using a garden spray and leave it to dry, 6–12 hours.

Wedge it out another 1 mm and wet it again.

If you do this three times the creases will be somewhat pulled out but never as good as a piece of uncreased cloth. The canvas will be rather taut as well.

Alternative to dipping the cloth in a bath

Instead of submerging the cloth in water you can stretch the canvas on to its chassis and spray it with water in a garden spray. Leave it to dry, approximately 6–12 hours. Once dry the cloth is removed and stretched again as normal.

This will prevent any creases occurring but will not fully shrink the cloth. The stretcher corners often make bulges in the cloth which do not come out and the weave of the cloth often goes wavy where it has been pulled by the staples as it shrank.

Other stretcher designs

The stretcher designs which are readily available are not ideal.

Readily available square-ended mortice and tenon joints are near to useless (fig. 12). When using the wedges, one side of each joint expands along the stretcher edge! Made with greater care, this corner design imposes the least tension on the canvas.

The self-tightening stretchers sold with primed canvas on, only save you hitting the wedges. You do still have to move the metal springs!

A more accentuated front bevel on the outer edge would prevent the inner edge of the stretcher bars showing as ridges on the front, either from priming or painting. A more rounded outer edge would also remove some of the long term stress on the canvas at this point. See fig. 13.

The non-rounded design could still be available for those who didn't like such a rounded edge. The joints could remain as tongue-and-grooved joints, although good mortice and tenons would be better. Artists may find stretcher makers or carpenters prepared to make such designs, or if you are a competent woodworker you can make your own. Some American designs already incorporate a front bevel.

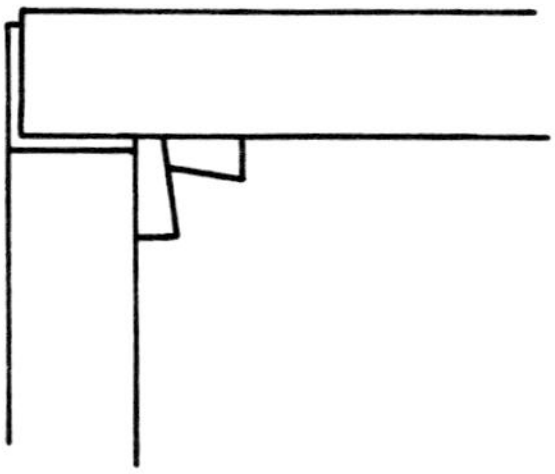

12. *Poorly made expanded mortice and tenon joint.*

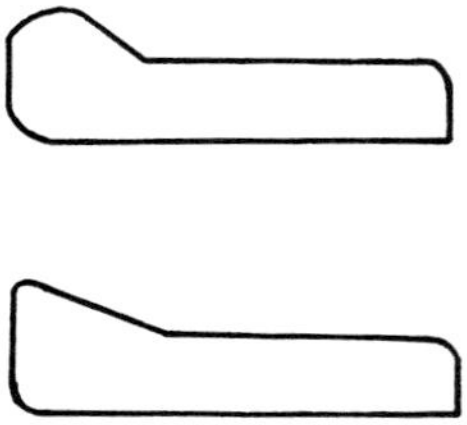

13. *Cross-section of two stretcher designs.*

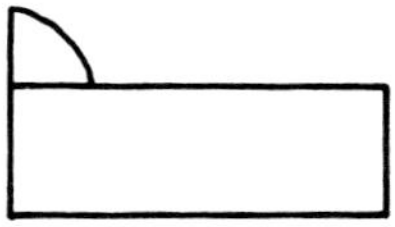

14. *Cross-section of stretcher showing beading.*

Making your own stretchers

Simple fixed stretchers can be made to save money on expandable ones (see fig. 72). Quadrangle beading can be added to fixed stretchers to act as a bevel (fig. 14).

Sizing canvas

Size is a glue used in a certain dilution to reduce the absorbency of a surface. It is employed in this case to stop the canvas absorbing any oil from the ground. Oil paint is destructive to its support and needs to be prevented from attacking it. Size does this by preventing oil being absorbed into the fibres, i.e. the strands which make up the cloth. Size should not fill the holes in the cloth itself. The ground has to be pushed into these holes later for structural reasons. A size therefore is never a continuous layer. The size used should be as flexible as possible and have the least possible hygroscopiscity. It needs to be flexible to endure the movement of the canvas which is actually increased by the size on it! The less hygroscopic it is, the less movement it will encourage of the canvas and the painting. Although it is far from meeting the above criteria, the most suitable glue is a rabbit-skin type. This means an animal glue made of skin and bones. Other possible sizes are acrylic sizes, sodium carboxy methyl cellulose (SCMC, SMC or CMC), and gelatin. Thorough research has yet to be done to establish which size is the best.

As size is a natural product it is not possible to give specific measurements. The measurements will be between 30–45 g ($1\frac{1}{2}$–$2\frac{1}{4}$ oz) of glue to 1.137 litres (2 pints) of water. The only way of knowing the right strength is to test the set of the cold size. 1.137 litres (2 pints) of size will be enough to cover a 122 × 183 cm (4 × 6′) canvas.

A double-boiler is used so that the glue is not scorched and is evenly distributed. Scorching or boiling size makes it brittle and reduces its pore-filling properties. Uneven distribution will mean some parts of the canvas will have too strong a sizing and other parts too weak. A double boiler can be any two pans, as long as there is water in the bottom one so that the size can be heated without it boiling.

If the size is too strong it will be too hygroscopic. Taken to the extreme, if the size has acted as a layer then the ground and painting can peel off! If the size is too weak the oil from the ground will sink into the cloth.

Making and using size

As a starting point put 40 g (2 oz) of glue with 1.137 litres (2 pints) of water into the top part of a clean double boiler.

When using a new bag of glue, make the initial batch by estimating the proportion of glue on the high side. It is quicker to adjust the glue if it is too strong than if it's too weak. This is because if you need to soak more granules in the prepared size it takes up to 12 hours for them to swell. Buy a big bag of glue and take note of the proportion of glue to water you need. Once you know the proportions that work for your bag you'll be able to make size quickly.

15. *RSG (rabbit-skin glue) granules and sheet.*

16. *Swollen granules in water.*

The granules will swell in the water to a uniform pale beige colour in approximately 2 hours. (Sheet glue can take 24 hours to swell and is more difficult to measure).

Once swollen, the glue is melted by heating in the double boiler. It melts in a few minutes. Leave the glue in a cool place to set. This can take between 2–10 hours. Keep the lid on the double boiler when possible throughout the process to prevent loss of water through evaporation. Test when it is at room temperature, otherwise it might appear stronger than it really is. When split with the finger the walls of the jelly should be uneven not smooth and if you mix the size up with your finger the resultant lumpy consistency should be that of apple sauce.

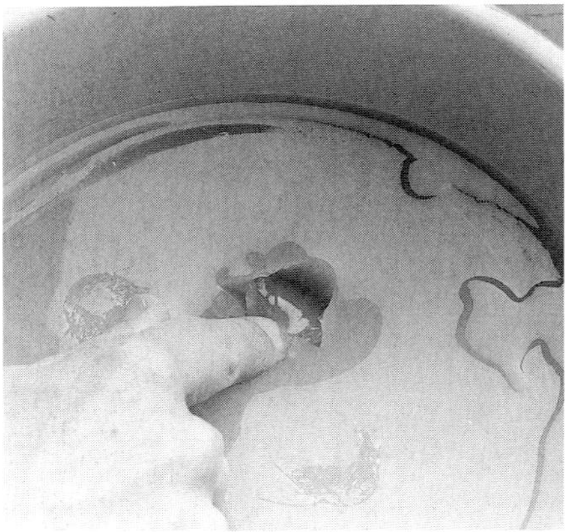

17. *Split size.*

18. *'Apple sauce' size.*

If the set is like consommé then it is too weak and needs some extra granules. If the set is like a fruit jelly then it is too strong and needs more water. Add whichever is necessary. If the size is too weak, add an extra 5–10 g ($\frac{1}{4}$ oz) of glue and leave to soak for at least 12 hours. If it's too strong add an extra 70–140 ml (up to $\frac{1}{4}$ pint) of water. Melt it again and leave to set. Repeat the process until you have the right set.

Continued heating reduces the strength of the size. Once you know the workable proportions for your bag of glue, the size should only need soaking, melting, setting, testing and reheating to use, i.e. only heated twice. Extra heating is probably unavoidable whilst you're learning. Also you may need to melt it more than twice in order to use it up on other stretched canvases. The size is applied hot. Heat it until it feels hot with your finger in it. Heat ensures even distribution. Use a 7 cm ($2\frac{3}{4}''$) varnishing brush for sizing; it doesn't flood the canvas with size, like a cheap decorator's brush does. Let the canvas absorb the size from a short brush stroke and then move on to the next bit of canvas. Do not make back and forth movements with your brush. It's wasted effort and too much size will be applied. Do not go over a wetted area again as too much size will be deposited. Cotton does not absorb the size like linen and it is often necessary to go over a patch again where the size has floated off. Just try to apply it evenly and sparingly.

Size the edges of the canvas as well as the painting plane. This will give you the same surface to paint on right up to and over the edge if required. Only one layer of size is necessary. More than one is similar to having too strong a size. Leave the canvas to dry flat naturally. This will take approximately 12 hours. After six hours or so, run your fingers gently round between the chassis and canvas to ensure none of the canvas has stuck to the stretcher.

Size will keep in the fridge for up to a week before beginning to decompose. Make sure size is fresh before use or make a new batch. The size will be watery and smelly if it's gone off. If the canvas is not flat when thoroughly dry, spray the canvas with water in a garden spray and leave it to dry again.

19. *Partly-sized canvas.*

Slubs and/or rough cloth

If you want to smooth the cloth and remove any small irregularities from it you can do so from the sized canvas with a scalpel blade and/or a pumice stone. The blade can slice off any slubs (little lumps of oversize thread) whilst a gentle rub over with the pumice will smooth the cloth. Don't be rough with the pumice as it can cut through the cloth!

Apply a second coat of size and leave to dry. This is necessary because of exposing more cloth fibres.

Sizing a board

Size all boards as for canvas except tempered hardboard which does not need sizing. Size both sides and the edges of an uncradled board in order to even up the hygroscopicity of the board and keep it flat. See gesso chapter (page 91) for explanation of sizing boards.

Canvas mounted on board

Canvas should be cut with enough overlap to fold over the edges of the board. It can be attached using canvas-strength size, but sticks better, particularly the overlap on the back, with gesso-strength size (see page 89). This also reduces the risk of blisters developing.

A cradled board is best because it will withstand the tension of the glued cloth on one side. Boards should be degreased and sanded (see page 89).

Coat the prepared board sparingly with hot glue on the face (and edges) which is going to receive the canvas. Place the prepared canvas on this surface with equal overlap all round. Ensure the weave of the cloth is parallel with the board. Glue the canvas down on the front with hot glue and a 7 cm ($2\frac{3}{4}''$) varnishing brush. Press it down with your fingers to ensure it is thoroughly glued down and no blisters can develop in the future. You can ensure there are no bubbles of cloth by looking across the board at eye level.

20. *Pressing canvas on to board.*

21. *Glued corner on reverse of board.*

22. *Canvas glued on board.*

Coat the edges and back of the board with hot glue where the overlap is to be glued down. Then fold the corners over the edge of the board in a similar way to using a chassis. This is more fiddly than corners on a chassis, especially on small boards, all corners will need to be folded before all the overlap can be glued down flat. Your fingers will be rather gluey too.

If using small uncradled boards, coat the whole reverse of the board, otherwise the board will warp. Leave to dry thoroughly, 6–12 hours.

Painting on sized canvas

Oil paintings on sized but not primed canvases have survived well and from this point of view they seem acceptable. They are more absorbent than primed canvas and produce quite a matt paint film. They should not be varnished (see page 38).

Sized but not primed canvases on open stretchers will tend to sag a lot. Use a paper backing as suggested (see page 29).

Painting on supports without sizing or priming

Use gelatin surface-sized rag paper of a reasonable weight or tempered hardboard. See *Index* to read more about either.

GROUNDS

A ground (primer) offers control of colour, texture and absorbency for the painting.

Oil paint becomes more and more transparent as it ages. If the ground is an opaque white then the maximum light is reflected back and the painting remains as bright as possible. In fact it will become brighter! If you do not want it to become brighter, a pale beige opaque coloured ground is the most suitable. See *Coloured grounds* (page 29).

A ground for oil paint must be lean. This is explained under *Fat over lean* (page 37).

The quicker the primer dries the better.

Oil grounds

Of oil, alkyd and acrylic grounds, an oil ground offers the most durable ground for oil paints. It can be used on canvas or board.

Linseed oil is used for grounds because it dries to a tougher, more flexible film than other drying oils.

White lead is the most suitable white pigment because it dries to a tough, flexible, lean film. It is also the quickest drying white pigment in oil. It is **toxic**. See *Health and safety* (page 9) and *Appendix B* (page 158) for keeping clean.

Its great disadvantage is that it takes up to six months to dry. When it is only touch dry it acts like a sponge and soaks up an enormous volume of paint. The painting will also crack later as the ground shrinks.

Titanium oil primer dries to a soft, chalky and fatter film than lead and takes at least as long to dry. Its whiteness makes it desirable in some cases.

Zinc is not used in oil grounds because it is the least opaque white and takes the longest to dry thoroughly.

Gesso grounds

Gesso offers a lean ground equally durable to an oil ground for oil paint. It can only be used on board or canvas on board and must be sized for oil paint. Its preparation time is about equal to an oil ground but it can be used within 36–48 hours. See gesso chapter (page 85).

Half chalk grounds

See gesso chapter, page 100.

Alkyd grounds, oil-modified alkyd resin

An alkyd is a synthetic resin. It is modified with a drying oil in order to produce a suitable film, hence oil-modified alkyd resin.

An alkyd ground is less durable than an oil ground. It may initially be flexible but embrittles with age. It may also yellow more. The pigment is titanium.

It will take at least 24 hours to dry thoroughly and may take up to a week. Painting on a touch-dry alkyd ground will have the same effect as a touch-dry oil ground. Rabbit-skin size is still required underneath.

Alkyd primer can be used on canvas or board.

After an oil ground and gesso, alkyd is the next most suitable ground for oil painting.

Acrylic grounds

Acrylic grounds are too fat (i.e. too flexible) for oil paint. See *Fat over lean*, page 37. Generally acrylic gesso primer is more absorbent than acrylic primer because it contains more chalk. Acrylic primers vary in absorbency from brand to brand. Sinking oil paint (ground too absorbent) results in dull, underbound and unmanageable paint and too little aborbency gives a slithery, equally unmanageable paint which can peel away from the ground at a later date from lack of adhesion. The pigment is titanium.

It is very quick drying, less than an hour for one coat! It is also used without applying rabbit-skin size because it does not adhere well to the canvas over it. It is this quick preparation which explains its popularity, both with artists and for many commercially primed canvases.

Acrylic primer can be used on canvas or board.

Acrylic emulsion remains soluble in the solvents which are used to clean oil paintings and therefore causes problems later.

Household paints and commercial primers

These products are made with acrylics and alkyds but are not made for fine artists and are likely to be far inferior to any of the above grounds. Without much understanding and information they should not be substituted for artists' primers.

Oil primer used over acrylic primer

This is not recommended because oil does not take well over acrylic. The effects and disavantages would be more or less the same as using an acrylic ground.

Preparing and using an oil ground

An oil primer of just the right slight absorbency can be made by mixing white lead primer with white spirit to the consistency of thick single cream. Just the correct absorbency will allow the oil paint to bite into the ground. Too much absorbency (too much thinners) will make the oil paint sink. Too little absorbency (not enough thinners) will make the oil paint slithery.

Oil paint is a poor adhesive. The structural durability of the ground and painting is ensured by driving the primer into the weave of the canvas where it can grip, i.e. into the holes in the cloth. On a board the primer can only grip the wood fibre.

The ground is applied as thin as possible. It is then more flexible and will dry more quickly and thoroughly.

An excellent brush for priming is a 115 mm ($4\frac{1}{2}''$) wavy mottler (fig. 25). They are stiff to help you drive the ground in and keep it thin and their width helps to spread the pressure of the priming.

The sized canvas will have a flat springy surface. In order to protect this a thin piece of card is placed between the stretcher and the canvas. This spreads the weight when you push the ground in and also prevents the inner edges of the stretcher bars showing on the front of the canvas.

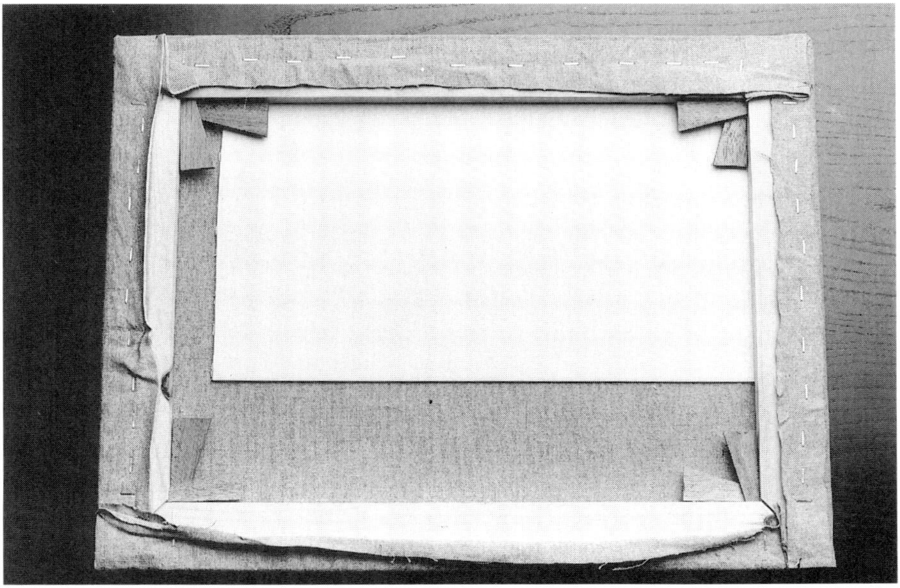

23. *Card in reverse of stretcher.*

24. *Thick single cream consistency of white lead primer.*

25. *Primer on wavy mottler brush.*

Four tablespoons of primer will be enough for approximately 122 × 183 cm (4 × 6′) canvas. Thin it to a thick single cream consistency. Using an old plate and spoon is easy. Don't put these back in the kitchen! Mix thoroughly so the thinners is dispersed. After approximately an hour the primer will thicken up from evaporation of thinners. Add more thinners if necessary to keep it at the right consistency.

Put a small amount of primer on the brush. Keep the brush upright and rub the ground into the weave of the cloth, thinning it out all the time. Complete each area before you move on. This saves time moving the card. Also you will have difficulty thinning out the primer once the thinners has evaporated.

Prime the edges of the canvas. Leave the canvas to dry in daylight for 6 months. Drying in excessive darkness or humidity will cause the canvas to darken. If this happens hang the canvas in daylight until it is bleached white.

26. *Oil primed canvas:* a. *weave not filled.* b. *correctly primed.*

Using alkyd primer

Size the canvas or board (see page 18). Do not thin the primer as it will become too absorbent. Apply one coat with the wavy mottler brush (see fig. 25). Leave to dry for 7 days.

Priming a board

The primer should be brushed on thinly with the wavy mottler, including the edges of the board. The colour of the board will not be masked because the primer is so thin. Using MDF which is lightest in colour of the wood fibre boards will help, or apply more coats of primer (below). Or you could resort to using plywood or blockboard, which are whiter than MDF (figs 70 and 71).

For the ultimate in bracing uncradled boards, paint a layer of primer on the reverse, followed by a layer of oil paint when the painting is made.

Priming canvas on board

Apply the primer as for canvas on an open chassis (see page 25).

One coat of primer versus two (single v. double priming)

One coat of primer is more flexible than two.

White lead primer is not particularly white and alkyd primer has poor covering power. Two coats in either case will make the canvas whiter and will fill in the weave of the cloth more. Apply the second coat of primer once the first coat is dry enough not to be picked up (3 days for white lead; 1 day for alkyd). A board may need more than two coats but any reduction in flexibility is negligible because the board is rigid. The difference in flexibility is not enough to deter you from using two coats on canvas if it suits you.

Controlling the sag of a canvas

When the ground is dry use the wedges to increase the tension of the canvas if it is not tight enough for you.

Using wedges

The left-side of the photo (fig. 28) shows the traditional way of putting in the wedges. This is to stop the wedges splitting down the grain as they are hit but it does make them very awkward to hit at all. Using them as in the right-hand side of the photo makes them easier to hit and in practice they rarely split.

Place a piece of card behind the wedges in each corner between the canvas and stretcher. This prevents you from denting the canvas accidentally with the hammer.

Always use the wedges by moving one stretcher bar at a time rather than splaying open a corner. This keeps the stretcher square.

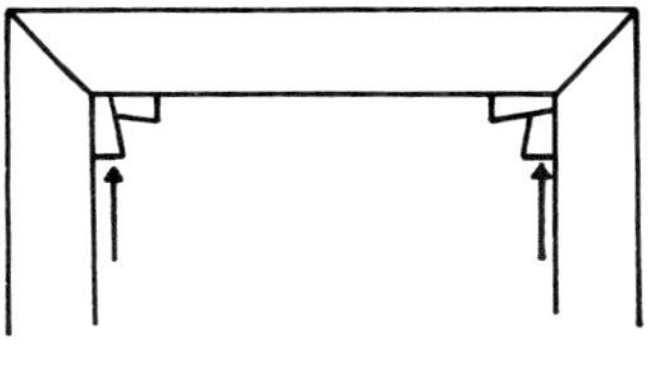

27. *Arrows indicate wedges which move out the horizontal stretcher bar.*

28. *Canvas corners showing traditional* (left) *and non-traditional* (right) *insertion of wedges.*

29. *Holding canvas whilst hammering in wedges. Pieces of card behind wedges to protect canvas.*

Stand the canvas upright and using a pin hammer, move the bar upwards whilst holding on to the vertical stretcher bars.

The stretcher bar will not move if you're holding it down with your hand! Move out the stretcher bars in succession until the canvas is flat. Usually the gap in the joints will be 1–2 mm ($\frac{1}{16}$").

30. *Paper on reverse of chassis protects canvas from changes in humidity.*

If a fixed chassis has been used you can try to tighten the canvas by removing the staples from one side or part of one side and stretching the canvas tighter. This is not easy. Canvas pliers might help, especially with cotton. Once as tight as you wish, staple a heavy (at least 200 gsm) sheet of paper or card over the back of the chassis. It is not desirable to make a tight seal between this backing and the chassis because that would encourage mould. The paper does not need to be acid free. This backing simply stabilizes the atmosphere immediately between the canvas and paper and makes the canvas far less susceptible to changes in humidity. It is the absorption of moisture by the size and canvas which makes the canvas sag. The less the paint film is relaxed and stretched, the smaller the chance of the painting developing cracks. This is much better than continually using the wedges to take up the slack of the canvas. That just puts more and more stress on the paint film as it is stretched by the tightening canvas.

A double stretched canvas would also make the painting less susceptible to humidity, i.e. one canvas is stretched, followed by another on top. The second canvas is then prepared as usual.

Canvases which are primed on both sides are also less susceptible to changes in moisture.

Saving money on priming

If you must make some cutbacks, it is better to have a good sizing and priming on cotton and a fixed stretcher (see *Other stretcher designs*, page 18) than to use household emulsion on linen. Cheaper still would be gesso on board.

Coloured grounds

There is no structural difference in coloured grounds. It is the optical differences that should be taken into consideration.

The optical advantage of the white ground can be retained by colouring the ground with a veil. This is a transparent colour which allows the light to travel through it to the white ground. The method is the same as for colouring a gesso board (see *Method i*, page 96), except that the veil does not need to be a second coat of size because the colour will not sink into the ground.

31. *Canvas with opaque coloured ground* (left) *and veiled ground* (right).

Opaque coloured grounds

The white ground can be coloured before thinning and application by mixing some oil colour into an oil ground or some alkyd paint into an alkyd ground. Because of its structural advantages, the ground should be coloured rather than replaced.

To maintain the structural advantage, keep the addition of paint to approximately 10%. This will produce a tinted ground which does not reflect back as much light as a veiled ground but can be used for coloured effects within the painting. The amount of white in the ground results in the ground being opaque. A pale beige ground is produced by this method. The dark toned grounds of previous centuries were made in this way. See *Bibliography* (page 171) for sources of further information on the colour effects of a ground.

Adding tooth to an oil or alkyd ground

Tooth can be added to a ground by mulling (page 30) a coarse inert pigment into the primer before applying it. Using ground instead of pigment on the slab add course pigment and mull it. See also *Other pigments* . . . (page 98) for suitable pigments. These pigments are also listed in full in the pigment list (page 131). Keep the addition of inert pigment to approximately 10% so that the ground retains its flexibility and other advantages.

Coloured and toothed grounds

Grounds can be coloured and toothed by a combination of both methods.

OIL PAINTS

Binder

Oil paints are bound with drying oils. A drying oil is a vegetable oil which dries by oxidization. Linseed oil is used in the majority of cases because it dries to the most durable film. The effects of different oils are discussed in *Making oil paint* (page 40). Also see the brand details, *Appendix A* (page 145) for the oils used.

Oil/resin paints are either oil/natural resin or alkyd resin paint. Both have different handling properties to conventional oil paint. The former should be durable provided the resin content is below 10%. More than that may cause yellowing and increased solubility of the paint film. See *Glaze mediums* (page 33) for those disadvantages. Oil/natural resin paints are not recommended for home manufacture. The manufacturer is experienced at controlling the quality of the binder, and heating oil and resin is a fire risk.

Alkyd paint should be durable but may tend to yellow more than conventional oil paint. See brand details, *Appendix A* (page 147) for details of oil/resin paints.

Water-soluble oil paints: There is only one make of these available at present. The binder is an emulsion of water and oil. They are claimed to be compatible with conventional oils. See brand details, *Appendix A*, page 146.

Oil paints in stick form are a mixture of linseed oil and wax. They are claimed to be compatible with conventional oil paint. See *Appendix A* (page 148) for brand details including any known information.

Pigments and the paint

Permanent pigments should be used. To establish the colours you want, use the pigment chapter (page 127) in conjunction with manufacturers' catalogues.

Note: Pigments which are sensitive to atmospheric pollution are substantially protected in oil by the binder and the subsequent picture varnish and can therefore be considered permanent in oil, e.g. flake white, ultramarine.

Please see *Discussion of artists' materials, particularly paints* ... about the quality of paints.

Some oil paints contain driers either to standardize drying rates or to contain some extremely slow driers. Drying times can be standardized to range between 2–10 days. Drying times for colours without driers will range from 2–30 days. See brand details, *Appendix A* (page 145) for brands with driers.

Making your own oil paint

Oil paint can be made by machine with less oil than is possible by hand, so in the extreme it will wrinkle and yellow less than any paint you can make yourself. However, do not let this deter you if for economic or aesthetic reasons you do want to make your own oil paint. Mixing the dry pigments together first will allow you to produce colours which normally have to be mixed on the palette. See *Making oil paint*, page 40.

USING OIL PAINT

Oil paint is at its optimum quality fresh from the tube. However in order to enjoy its possibilities we have to accept some further additions to it as necessary evils. The important thing is to resist letting any of these additions become the dominant part of your oil technique, e.g. impasto, or glaze medium.

Thinners

The thinners for oil paint are turpentine or white spirit.

Turpentine is distilled from the sap of pine trees (a distilled oleoresin).

Turpentine will oxidize, leaving a gummy residue which yellows badly and leaves the oil paint sticky and non-drying. To reduce the risk of this, use only double-distilled or rectified turpentine as sold by art materials suppliers (see page 168). Leaving some turpentine to evaporate on a palette will show if it leaves a gummy residue. Storing turpentine in half-empty bottles and in daylight will cause oxidization. Try to use turpentine up quickly or store in full, dark, capped bottles.

White spirit (also mineral spirits, odourless paint thinner) is a petrol distillate which does not oxidize. Although buying artists' grade is not necessary, you should buy a white spirit with a BS (British Standard) on the container. Turpentine substitue does not conform to a BS.

Both turpentine and white spirit are toxic. See *Health and safety* (page 9).

White spirit is significantly cheaper than turpentine.

Turpentine can be reserved for use if you find it easier to manipulate, prefer the smell, or if it is needed as a superior solvent to white spirit. It is slower drying and more viscous than white spirit.

Using thinners

Thinners should not be used to thin the paint to a water-like consistency. This will prevent any oil film forming because it has been thinned to the extreme and the pigment will be left under/un-bound on the ground. If a stain is required, paint on the water-like paint and then immediately rub it off with a rag. This will leave a stain without loose pigment. If you find yourself wanting this effect often, consider using tempera or watercolour!

Matt oil painting

Using white spirit to effect mattness can thin the paint too much and give uneven mattness across the painting. For a thin matt painting, using a sized but not primed canvas may be more effective (see page 23). For a heavier matt painting, using wax is possible. See *Impasto*, page 33.

Using an absorbent ground e.g. unsized gesso is not recommended for achieving mattness because the pigment would be left underbound on the surface.

The easiest way to achieve an even, matt oil painting is to varnish it with a matt removable picture varnish when the painting is dry. Using a spray gun will give a fine layer which will matt the painting but not show as a varnish layer. See *Varnishing*, page 38.

Economical use of thinners

Thinners can be used in a wide-lipped jar or tin, replacing the lid at the end of the painting session. By the next day, most of the pigment will have settled at the bottom and you can decant the thinners into another tin. The first can be wiped clean for the following session, and so on. The thinners can be topped up as needed. Dispose of solvent-soaked rags safely, not on an open fire.

Gradation of layers

When building up an oil painting, each underlayer will absorb oil from the paint of each subsequent layer. In the extreme this will be very noticeable in sunken patches. If time is no object, careful oiling out between layers will prevent subsequent layers being weakened. See *Oiling out*, page 36. As time is usually a consideration, the thinners can include some oil instead. Approximately 10% stand oil should be used in white spirit. Up to 50% can be used, if with experience 10% is not enough. Stand oil is used because it is non-yellowing. This also goes some way towards keeping the 'fat over lean' rule (see page 37).

Glaze mediums

A glaze is a transparent layer/s built up over dry underlayers, which results in a spatial atmospheric surface. A glaze medium provides a reflective surface which contributes further to this effect.

The glaze medium can also be used as an additional dilutent for oil paint giving an inner glow to the paint.

Glaze mediums are most effective when they use a mixture of oil, varnish and thinners; although, stand oil and thinners will produce a more stable structure.

Glaze medium
1 part stand oil
1 part (or less) ketone gloss (or damar) varnish
5 parts white spirit

Using one fluid ounce as one part will make a jar full of medium. Keep lid on the medium, decanting a small amount at a time, otherwise the solvent will evaporate.

See *List of sources*, page 163.

Ketone resin gives the glassy effect to the glaze and is non-yellowing in itself. Ketone varnish should be used sparingly and never without the stand oil because of its solubility in thinners, i.e. subsequent layers of paint could dissolve previous ones which contained a lot of ketone. That would not only make it difficult to paint and varnish but very difficult to clean such pictures. Its solubility is partly inhibited by the stand oil.

Type of resin

Ketone varnish is water white, whilst **damar** varnish is pale yellow. Ketone varnish is suggested because it does not yellow like damar and does not contain turpentine. No results are yet known to be more satisfactory in the long run than from the use of damar. Neither resins are satisfactory ingredients in an oil paint film, but essential for the glaze effect.

Alkyd resin tends to yellow, so is not an ideal substitute.

Keeping the use of a glaze medium to a minimum is the best advice.

Stand oil levels extremely well, i.e. it does not hold brushmarks. It adds elasticity which compensates for any brittleness of the ketone and it is pale and non-yellowing.

Commercial mediums can contain unsatisfactory ingredients. Check ingredients in manufacturers' catalogues before use.

Do not mix mediums within one painting because an over-complicated weak structure would result.

See end of this chapter for notes on other ingredients/mediums.

Impasto

Oil paint was not designed to be used as a heavy impasto technique. You should consider acrylic or encaustic; or sculptural pieces can be made out of wood, gessoed and then oil painted over the top; all are more durable than using oil paint for impasto.

If necessary, beeswax paste is the safest impasto medium. Mix it well into the oil paint on the palette with a palette knife. It will however make the oil paint susceptible to heat, denting, and scuffing, and will make the paint matt and slower drying.

Melt 28 g (1 oz) of yellow beeswax in a double boiler. Once liquid, move the wax away from the heat because of the fire risk. Stir in 100 ml ($3\frac{1}{2}$ fl.oz) of turpentine or 70 ml ($2\frac{1}{2}$ fl.oz) of white spirit. Stir until the wax cools and a paste is formed. Keep a lid on this medium to prevent the evaporation of the solvent. Turpentine is a better solvent and is slower drying than white spirit, but see page 31 for full information on turpentine and white spirit. Also see page 53 for full information on beeswax and page 43 for alternative mediums.

Drying rates of oil colours and their effect on painting

Oil paints which are slow driers should be avoided in underpainting because the underlayers will remain mobile and move as they dry. This causes cracking of the fast drying colours which may be used on top of them. This is also true of colours which only surface dry, like cobalt.

Colours ground in poppy or similar oils should be avoided in underpainting for this reason. See page 40 for further information on oils and *Appendix A* (page 145) for brand details.

An underpainting white, alkyd white or flake white (in linseed oil) is recommended in underpainting because of their quick and thorough drying.

Paintings made in layers are also less likely to crack if the underpainting is thinly applied i.e. a thin paint film, not an excessively *thinned* paint film. It then has more chance to dry thoroughly.

The following list gives a guide to the drying rates of pigments in linseed oil. The categories may be somewhat approximate due to different makes of pigments or different test methods.

All colours made with poppy oil will dry relatively slower than in the list. See brand details, *Appendix A*, page 145.

The paint ranges which contain driers will reflect the list below more moderately because an effort has been made to make all the colours average driers.

Rapid driers: Aureolin, flake white, manganese black, umbers.

Rapid/average driers: Chrome green, chrome yellows and oranges, cobalt blue, manganese blue, manganese violet, nickel azo yellow, phthalocyanine blue, siennas.

Average driers: Barium yellow, burnt green earth, chromium oxide green, cobalt green, cobalt violet, Mars colours, Naples yellow, phthalocyanine green, quinacridones, some natural iron oxides, strontium yellow, ultramarine violet, viridian, whiting, zinc yellow.

Slow driers: Alizarin crimson, cerulean, green earth, some natural iron oxides, ultramarine blue, yellow ochre.

Slow/very slow driers: Hansa yellow, lapis lazuli, lithopone, rose madder, titanium yellow.

Very slow driers: Alumina hydrate, cadmium colours, ivory black, lamp black, Vandyke brown, vermilion, zinc oxide.

Speeding the drying rate

The safest way to accelerate the drying rate of certain colours is to use sun-thickened linseed oil or a proprietary mixture of oil with driers. See *List of sources* (page 165). Neat driers (e.g. cobalt) are not recommended because they can crack the paint. The safe addition of driers depends on each pigment and is best left to the experience of manufacturers.

Retarding the drying rate

To retard the drying rate of oil paint, use a 50:50 stand oil and white spirit mixture to thin with. Alternatively, try using Blockx paint which is made mostly of poppy oil and therefore dries altogether more slowly. See *Appendix A* (page 145) for brand details and *List of sources* (page 165). Oil of cloves is not recommended, it has a tendency to blacken and affect the stability of the paint film.

NOTE ON THE THREE WHITES FOR OIL PAINT

See also pigment list, page 127.

Because it dries to a tough, flexible and lean film, flake white is the best general white for oil paint. If used throughout the painting the whole painting will become more tough and flexible. Flake white also brushes out more smoothly than titanium or zinc. It is rarely affected by atmospheric pollution because of the protection of the binder and picture varnish. **Toxicity** is dealt with in the pigment chapter (page 129) and *Health and safety* (page 9). It is the least white of the three pigments and is semi-opaque. Also see pages 34, 38, 40, 165 for uses of flake white in underpainting.

Titanium dries to a soft, chalky and fatter film in oil which can be further weakened by the oil and pigment separating. It is the whitest and most opaque of the three pigments. It should be used where a brighter, more opaque white is needed.

Zinc dries to a hard, brittle and lean film in oil. It is a bluer white than titanium but whiter than flake and is semi-opaque. It should be used where a more transparent white is needed.

Mixed whites can be used when a combination of pigments is desirable. The characteristics and advantages of the three whites are too individual for a mixed white to serve all purposes.

NOTES ON PROBLEMS WHEN USING OIL PAINT

Sinking oil paint, retouch varnish and oiling out

If your paint is sinking, ensure that your ground is of the correct type and dry.

Spots of dull paint across the canvas are due either to areas of thin paint or new paint over touch-dry paint, the latter sucks the oil from the new paint like a sponge.

Although varnishing the finished picture will produce an even matt or gloss over the picture, it is more stable and desirable to stop any further sinking during painting.

Retouch varnish should be used if you need a quick solution. Retouch is a non-water-based size. It reduces the absorbency of the oil paint already on the canvas but does not prevent the subsequent layer of paint gripping it. Retouch does present some risk of solvent action (see page 33).

Use a soft brush and paint on a thin layer of retouch to the required area and leave to dry, approximately 5–15 minutes. Use more than one layer if sinking still occurs. Three thin layers are structurally safer than one thick one. Allow the retouch to dry before overpainting, otherwise subsequent paint layers may remain tacky.

Oiling out is the safest way of preventing further sinking. There is no risk of solvent action but it is not a quick solution.

Oiling out replaces the oil which the underlayer has sucked out of the top layer. Use an 80:20 stand oil/white spirit solution. Rub it sparingly into the sunken areas with a soft lint-free cloth (i.e. the cloth must not leave fluffy bits) and leave for 24 hours. After that period wipe off any excess oil and leave to dry for a week. An excess of oil will prevent new paint gripping old and will also yellow more. If the areas are still sunken, repeat the process. Stand oil is used because it is non-yellowing.

Overpainting dry pictures

You may find when you go back to a part of the picture which is dry that the dry paint is somewhat resistant to the new wet paint. Use the oiling out procedure to bond the old and new paint together. A rubber should not be used because it will leave a deposit which will interfere with the paint film.

Matching wet colours to dry

Wet colours can be matched to any dry colours already on the canvas either by oiling out or by using retouch on the dry paint. The oil or retouch will gloss the paint again as if it were still wet (see page 35).

METHODS NOT RECOMMENDED WITH OIL PAINT

Half-dry paint and storing exposed oil paint

Once oil paint is exposed on the palette it starts to oxidize. Half-dry paint will not adhere to the canvas to produce a stable film in the way fresh paint does. Keep your palette clean and once the fresh paint needs an excess of thinners to revive it or if it feels gummy then discard it. Rubbery lumps or hardened paint out of the tube should not be used either.

Keeping oil paint under water will not prevent it oxidizing. It can still oxidize using the oxygen from the water, and water residue in the paint can disturb the stability of the paint film. If anything, keeping it under oil would be more sensible.

Tins of paint are only really economical if you use up all the paint quickly.

Oily paint

Any paint which is just too oily can be dried off by leaving it on paper for a couple of minutes. Excess oil will be absorbed by the paper.

Using old canvases

This is not recommended because the old oil painting will show through eventually as the paint becomes more transparent (pentimento) and the structure is bound to be overcomplicated and weak. The preparation of an old canvas is a waste of time, it will never behave like a new one. Commercial paint strippers deposit grease and solvent which prevent primer and oil paint taking on the cleaned canvas.

However, if the paint is still wet or just touch dry, you could scrape it off back to the ground with a palette knife. This will provide a perfectly suitable surface to paint on but it will be stained from the previous paint.

Manageable-sized pieces of canvas which were originally sized could be submerged in hot water and left to soak for half an hour to see if the priming and painting will peel off as the size dissolves. The canvas could then be reused.

Removing canvases from stretchers

A chassis should not be reused unless you have scrapped the canvas which was on it. It is tedious to re-stretch finished paintings and an expandable stretcher is the only way to achieve a flat canvas again.

Oil paintings are not flexible enough to withstand rolling. If you are going to roll canvases, then do so with the picture on the outside, using as large a diameter tube as possible to roll it on to. Any cracks will then fold in on themselves. Do not roll oil paintings on paper.

FAT OVER LEAN

Fat over lean can be paralleled with flexible over inflexible.

If an inflexible coat is laid over a flexible one, then as the flexible coat moves the inflexible one will split. However if the situation were reversed, then as the inflexible one moves less than the flexible coat on top of it, the latter will not split. This of course applies to grounds as well. This is why a lean ground is needed for oil paint.

One of the varying properties which pigments have, is the different amount of oil they absorb to make a usable paint. Paints which contain a lot of oil can be classed as 'fat' whilst paints which contain little oil can be termed 'lean'. A fat colour can contain several times as much oil as a lean colour. Practically, the matter comes down to the following points:

If the picture is completed in one session when all the paint is wet then oil content need not be considered.

When a picture is painted in layers, the only way to prevent subsequent layers of paint from cracking is to avoid painting with high oil content colours in the under-painting. Adding oil to thinners will not prevent lean colours from cracking if they are applied over fat ones.

The following list gives a guide to some of the high oil content colours which should be avoided in underpainting. This list is somewhat approximate because different batches of the same colour can absorb different amounts of oil. Oil paints which contain extenders and/or stabilizers (see *Appendix A*, page 145) will vary somewhat in absorption rates because of the inert pigments or waxes added to them.

High oil content colours (paints)
Alizarin crimson, aureolin, cadmium orange, cobalt blue, ivory black, lamp black, manganese violet, phthalocyanines, quinacridones, viridian.

Paints made with synthetic organic pigments tend to be fat.

Flake white, ground in linseed oil, or an underpainting or alkyd white is recommended in underpainting because of its leanness (see *Appendix A*, page 145). High oil content colours can safely be used to tint white in underpainting.

Paintings made in layers are also less likely to crack if the underpainting is thinly applied, i.e. the paint film is thin, not excessively thinned.

CARE OF FINISHED OIL PAINTINGS

A finished oil painting should be left to dry in a light, dry atmosphere as in priming canvas (see page 26). If it hasn't been and permanent oil colours were used then the darkened oil can be bleached by normal daylight. Bad luck if you used fugitive colours!

Protection from pollution
A dried oil film attracts dirt and grease. If it is left unprotected, the dirt ingrains itself and dulls the picture irreversibly. Only oil paintings which are packed away from general life can be left unprotected. If the picture is to be hung then it should be varnished or put in a glazed frame. See *Appendix C* (page 160) for framing pictures.

Producing an even sheen
Using varnish will produce an even matt or gloss over a picture, covering any uneven effects from sinking, variation in colour, paint handling etc.

Varnishing oil paintings

Drying time for oil paintings
An oil painting will not be dry enough to varnish for at least a year after it is finished. It must be dry before being varnished or it is likely to crack or ripple as it shrinks or expands under the varnish.

In emergency
If the picture must be shown and needs an even sheen, either oil out or apply retouch to sunken areas. See *Sinking oil paint* (page 35). A proper application of picture varnish should be applied after the usual drying time.

Varnishing paintings on sized but unprimed canvas and other delicate paint films
These paintings should not be varnished because the varnish will soak into them too much and its attempted removal when dirty will damage the paint film. Instead, these paintings should be hung in glazed frames. See *Appendix C* (page 160).

Varnishes

Picture varnish must always be removable. It collects pollution like the oil film and is removed and replaced when dirty.

Ketone resin varnishes are recommended because they do not yellow as fast as natural resin varnishes (damar and mastic) and they do not bloom. Both matt and gloss varnishes are available, or you can mix the two for something in between.

Wax picture varnishes are acceptable but they will need replacing far sooner than a ketone varnish. Wax varnishes are matt.

Acrylic resin varnishes are also acceptable. However, do make sure that you are sold a 'removable picture varnish' for oil painting and not an acrylic 'medium'. There can be some confusion. A medium could prove difficult to remove when dirty. Acrylic varnishes come in gloss and matt and can be mixed.

Varnishing

Using a soft rag and some white spirit, test an area of the painting to ensure it is dry enough to varnish. If anything more than a trace of colour comes off, the painting must be left longer to dry.

Any dirt or dust which has accumulated whilst the painting has been drying should be removed. Use a soft cloth dampened with water. There should not be enough water to deposit a residue on the painting.

Varnish in a well ventilated dry and dust-free atmosphere. Leave the painting and the varnish together to acclimatize for several hours prior to varnishing. Do not attempt to varnish on a damp day; it's bound to fail because moisture and varnish don't mix!

Use a dry 7 cm ($2\frac{3}{4}''$) varnishing brush. Thin the varnish if necessary in order for it to brush out thinly and smoothly. A spray gun can be used to apply very thin layers of varnish. Dilute the varnish as necessary to get it through the gun. A spray gun is excellent for getting an even sheen. Do not use a mouth atomiser because you will introduce moisture from your mouth into the varnish. You must protect your skin and eyes and prevent inhaling the spray when using a spray gun. See *Health and safety*, page 9.

Apply the varnish with the painting horizontal. Keep the coat thin and repeat it at right angles if the painting does not look evenly covered. In 15 minutes the varnish will have set and the picture can be leant face-inwards against a wall to prevent dust settling on it whilst it dries.

Wash the brush with white spirit as suggested in *Appendix B* (page 159).

After using a spray gun, clean it with white spirit. Pump it through the gun, to clean the nozzle thoroughly. Dried varnish within the nozzle is much harder to remove than fresh varnish.

Removing dents from canvases

If you accidentally dent a canvas, moisten the dented area sparingly on the back of the canvas. Use water in a garden spray or dab water on with your finger. Don't rub the canvas because you could disturb the size. Leave to dry and the dent should flatten out.

MAKING OIL PAINT

Making and using oil paint within a few months avoids the need for stabilizers.

To achieve a stable paint, pigment particles must be evenly dispersed in binder.

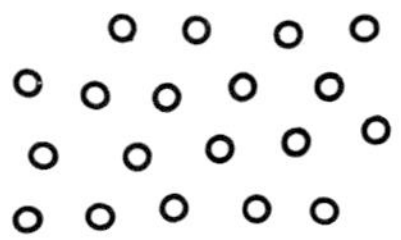

32. *Pigment particles evenly dispersed in binder.*

Oils

Cold-pressed linseed oil (sometimes called grinding oil) is recommended for hand grinding because it maximizes the wetting and dispersing of pigment particles in oil.

Refined linseed oil can be used but it does not wet nor disperse the pigment so easily.

It is debatable how different in flexibility and yellowing are these two types of oil; but they are both undoubtedly more suitable than any of the other oils.

Sun-thickened, sun-refined or sun-bleached linseed oil dries faster but is less flexible and yellows more than either of the above.

Bodied, blown or boiled oils have the same characteristics as sun-treated oils but embrittle and yellow more.

Stand oil will remain more flexible and non-yellowing than other oils but is a slow dryer.

All these oils have reduced wetting and dispersing properties compared to cold-pressed linseed oil.

Raw linseed oil is too dark and poorly processed to be used in painting.

Refined poppy oil is slower drying and less yellow than linseed but has a tendency to crack. It should not be used for colours in underpainting because of this. It is often used in whites, and sometimes in blues and pale colours because it is so pale itself. If using poppy oil colours, it is safer to complete the painting in one layer. Used in overpainting the risk of cracking is smaller. An underpainting white, alkyd white or flake white, ground in linseed oil, is recommended for underpainting (see *Appendix A*, page 145).

Poppy oil gives a short (buttery) consistency to an oil paint. This can be useful instead of using other stabilizers for colours which tend to be stringy (see list, page 41). Using up to 20% of poppy oil with linseed oil will not display the disadvantages of poppy oil and should be enough to somewhat shorten the consistency of these colours.

Safflower oil has similar characteristics and uses to poppy oil but does not exhibit the disadvantages to the same degree.

Sunflower oil is also used instead of poppy or safflower.

Walnut oil has been popular in the past but it has no overall advantages over linseed or poppy.

Pigments

Pigments can be chosen for their lightfastness, drying time, oil absorption or opacity. See the pigment chapter (page 127) and the oil chapter (pages 34, 38).

A suitable respirator should be used when handling dry pigments. See *Health and safety*, page 9.

Making the paint

Because of the varying weights and oil absorptions of pigments it is only possible to approximate how much pigment is needed to make a tube of oil paint. About 100 g ($3\frac{1}{2}$ oz) of pigment should fill a 150 ml (5 fl. oz) tube.

Place the pigment on the slab (plate) and make a well in the centre. Pour in just enough oil to mix it to a stiff paste with a palette knife as in fig. 47. Try to keep the oil to a minimum. An excess of oil produces a weaker and more yellowing paint which is more likely to wrinkle.

Some pigments will resist being wet by the oil. You just have to keep going. You could stabilize these colours with wax if continued mixing and grinding really doesn't help.

Mull the paste until you have a smooth oil paint. Periodically stop and scrape the paste back into the centre of the slab and off the muller using a large palette knife or paint scraper. See photograph, fig. 49. As the pigment disperses, the paste will loosen up to a normal paint consistency. This could take between 10 and 60 minutes!

Clean the muller and plate as suggested in *Appendix B*, page 159.

Overgrinding oil paint

When pigments are ground into very fine particles the colour can be 'killed'. It is extremely unlikely that you could manage this by hand!

Stringy Pigments

Some pigments make stringy/sticky paint, e.g. ultramarine, viridian, zinc white and some yellow ochres. If you don't like it try the following:

Leave the mulled pigment to relax for 6–12 hours. Then mix more pigment in and re-mull it. This packing can reduce stringyness. Do not make the paint too stiff or there will be a lack of oil in it. Common sense will tell you when the paint is fully packed. Alternatively, you could try substituting poppy oil for some of the linseed oil. Try 10% first, only adding more if necessary.

Stabilizing colours

Some pigments are apt to separate from the oil. The longer the paint is kept the more likely this is to happen, e.g. chromium oxide green, titanium white.

Other pigments are gritty and are easier to grind and disperse if wax is substituted for some of the oil, e.g. aureolin, cobalt green, prussian blue, viridian.

Yellow beeswax melted into the oil will act as a stabilizer in both cases. See page 53 for full information on beeswax. Beeswax, 2% by volume is recommended because the more wax there is, the higher the oil absorption of the pigments, the more the colour strength of the pigment is reduced, and the softer and less durable the paint film will be. Measure 114 ml (4 fl.oz) of oil and 3 g of wax for a 2% volume of wax. If a pigment does not respond to 2% beeswax, try adding up to another 2%, but never go beyond a total of 4% wax by volume.

Use a double boiler when melting the beeswax into the oil and be careful as both substances are a fire hazard when heated. Prevent water splashing into the oil which would lead to an unstable paint film.

Do **not** add water to smooth and stiffen oil paint because it will make the paint go hard in the tube and produce a particularly unstable paint film.

Filling the empty tubes

Loosen the lid of the tube so that air can escape as you fill it. Use a thin palette knife to shovel the paint into the tube. Whilst holding the tube upright, occasionally tap the tube on the table to settle the paint and to prevent air from being trapped in the tube with the paint. Tap the tube gently on the table or you may squash it. Fill it until there is approximately 25 mm (1″) of the tube left empty at the open end. Flatten the tube approximately 30–40 mm ($1\frac{1}{4}$–$1\frac{1}{2}$″) from the end so that a little paint and all the air oozes out. Wipe the tube clean with a rag.

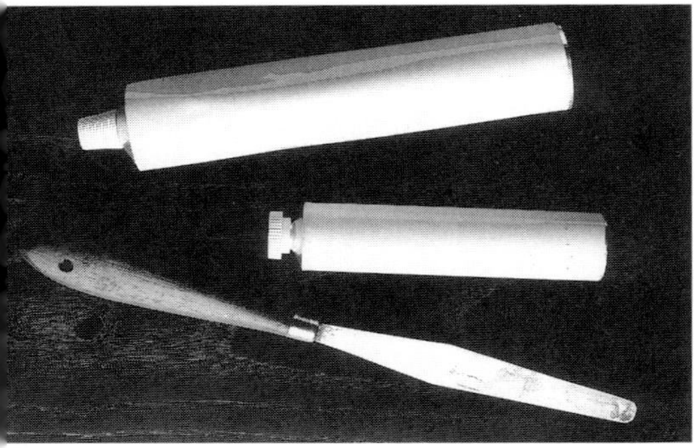

33. *Empty tubes and palette knife.*

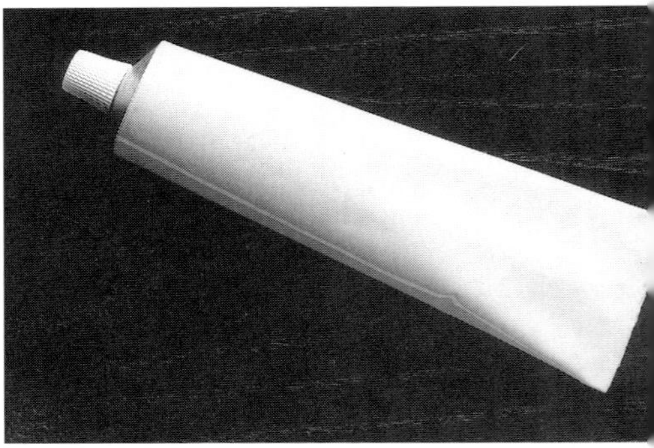

34. *Flattened tube.*

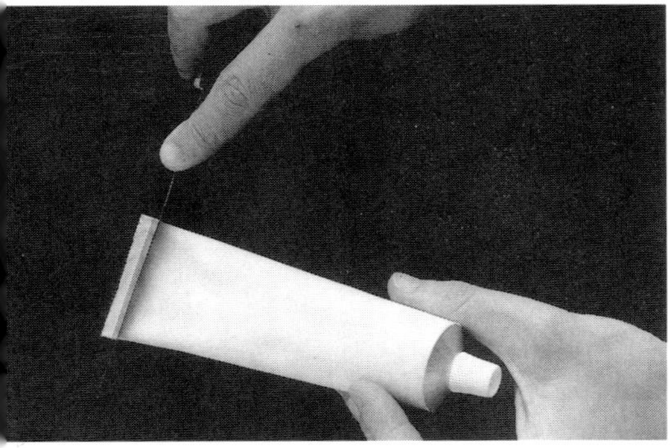

35. *Folding tube with palette knife.*

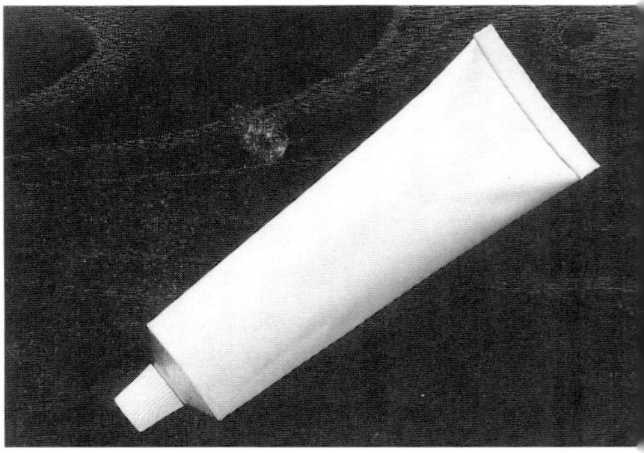

36. *Sealed tube of paint.*

Use a palette knife to fold the end of the tube. Make two folds so the end is totally enclosed.

ALTERNATIVE INGREDIENTS FOR OIL MEDIUMS

Mediums should not be mixed within one painting because an over complicated, unstable structure would result.

Other oils in glaze mediums
Sun-treated oil is a quicker drier than stand oil and levels well but it yellows much more than stand oil. Cold-pressed and refined oils are not pale yellow and do not have good levelling properties.

Oleoresins or balsams
These are mixtures of an essential oil and resin from trees, including Venice turpentine, Strasburg turpentine, Canada balsam, copaiba balsam.

Used for glazing in the past. They tend to darken and crack and are expensive.

Oil varnishes
These are made of a resin heated and melted in a drying oil. They include amber, burgundy pitch, copal (all types), elemi, kauri, mastic (meglip), rosin (colophony), and sandarac. They produce both dark and pale varnishes for mediums and are not recommended because of their tendency to darken. This tendency is mostly due to poor quality resin.

Meglip can also wrinkle, crack, blister and behave altogether erratically.

Oil modified alkyd resin
A synthetic resin, modified with a drying oil, soluble in white spirit and turpentine. Usually available under trade names for impasto and glaze mediums.

Alkyd resin appears to embrittle and turn yellow/brown. Excessive use can cause the paint to sheer off. Beeswax appears to be a more durable impasto medium.

Other waxes
Microcrystalline wax is a possible substitute for beeswax. We do not yet know how flexible and non-yellowing it remains. Paraffin waxes are not recommended because they yellow and embrittle.

Shellac
A resin from insects, shellac should not be used in oil painting because it embrittles and darkens. The bleached type will darken less.

Oil of spike lavender
Similar to turpentine but it has a greater tendency to gum and oxidize and is therefore better replaced by turpentine.

Asphaltum
Entered in the pigment list (see page 131).

See *Bibliography* (page 171) for sources of other information.

UNDERPAINTING

Underpainting with tempera paint

Tempera allows you to make a preliminary/under painting which dries rapidly. Egg tempera is best because it is not picked up when the oil paint is subsequently applied. The oil paint should be applied as soon as possible after the tempera is complete, i.e. within a couple of months at the most. The adhesion between the two mediums is best whilst the egg emulsion is still soft and slightly absorbent. This technique would be most stable on gesso because of the inflexibility of the tempera and the lack of absorbency of other grounds.

Underpainting with alkyd paint

Alkyd paint also allows you to make a preliminary under painting which dries rapidly. See pages 30, 147.

Underpainting with acrylic paint

Underpainting with acrylic paint is not recommended for oil painting for the same reasons as using acrylic grounds (see page 24). Alkyd or tempera are better suited to underpainting for oil paints.

USING TEMPERA OVER WET OIL PAINT

For occasional crisp effects see tempera chapter, page 70.

Chapter 2
ACRYLIC PAINTING

Acrylic is a quick drying, insoluble medium which can be used thickly or thinly, opaquely or transparently, with variable gloss/mattness and can be used without a ground. Acrylic is an excellent paint for impasto as thick layers will not crack like oil paint, although, overall, an acrylic painting is less robust than a sound oil painting.

The emulsion is an adhesive so acrylic is a suitable paint to make collages and mixed media with.

Acrylic has the largest variety of safe mediums.

Acrylic painting can be resumed at any time but the paint cannot be removed once it is dry.

When using acrylic products either use everything from one brand or test before mixing. Some emulsions do not produce a stable mixture or adhere to one another. If any mixtures blister, bubble or peel they should not be used together.

Gradation of layers

Acrylic paint is more or less equal in strength and flexibility regardless of the pigment. It is therefore possible for any colour to be used for priming or on top of one another. This is in reference to requirements in other media.

SUPPORTS

The acrylic paint film itself is not destructive to its support and movement of the support affects acrylic paint less than oil.

Acrylic will adhere to anything which is clean, non-greasy and has some sort of key.

A ground is only necessary to manipulate the colour, texture or absorbency of the support.

Canvas: See oil chapter (page 11) for types of canvas.

Polyester can be used for acrylics provided it is untreated. Cloths made for boats and clothing are dressed with resins which reduce their key for paint. Other synthetic cloths offer poor paint adhesion.

Boards can be used if a hard, weaveless surface is desired. See gesso chapter (page 85) for types of board, their preparation and construction.

Plywood and blockboard are less likely to transfer hairline cracks through the painting because acrylic is more flexible than gesso.

Paper is a good support for acrylics. Rag paper is recommended.

See paper chapter (page 102).

Other supports include aluminium, steel, copper, glass fibre, leather, parchment, vellum, marble, slate, ivory.

See *Bibliography* (page 171) for sources on preparation.

Preparation of supports

Canvas can be stretched on stretchers or on to a board. See oil chapter (pages 14, 22).

Canvas should still be dipped as under *Initial preparation of canvas* (page 13). Acrylic ground/paint is water-based so would still shrink the canvas.

Acrylic ground/paint will not stretch the canvas as rabbit-skin size does. The canvas will only tighten slightly as the ground dries.

The canvas should be stretched to make it flat but make sure the weave remains parallel with the stretcher bars. The canvas can also be tightened after priming by using the wedges. See oil chapter (page 27).

Note: Use acrylic emulsion instead of rabbit-skin glue to stick canvas on to board. This makes for a more sympathetic structure. Dilute the emulsion with approximately 20% water. Otherwise it dries too quickly, fills in the weave of the canvas and doesn't glue the canvas down efficiently. Press the canvas down well with your fingers to ensure no blisters develop in the future. Leave to dry thoroughly, approximately 3–10 hours, before applying ground.

Boards should be degreased and sanded. Acrylic will not take well over greasy boards. See gesso chapter (page 89). Boards larger than 60 cm (24″) square need to be mounted on a chassis. See gesso chapter (page 87).

Paper needs to be stretched if any vigorous or sustained painting is intended. See watercolour chapter (page 74).

Absorbency of supports

Acrylic grounds can be directly applied to canvas or paper.

Boards made of wood fibre may be too absorbent. If you experience any problems with sinking paint or weak, crumbly paint films, the support should be sized, i.e. the support is sucking too much binder from the paint and leaving the pigment underbound on the surface.

This sizing is not done with rabbit-skin glue because the acrylic does not adhere to its support with rabbit-skin glue in between. Diluted acrylic emulsion is used instead.

Sizing boards and gesso

Use acrylic emulsion diluted with approximately 30–50% water. This depends on the degree to which you want to reduce the absorbency.

MDF, hardboard and Sundeala are likely to need a strongish size, i.e. approximately 30% water; whilst gesso, hardwood and canvas are likely to need a weaker one, i.e. approximately 50% water.

Brush it sparingly on the face and edges with a 7 cm ($2\frac{3}{4}$″) varnishing brush and leave to dry flat. If using an uncradled board, turn it over once it is dry enough and size the other side. Leave to dry thoroughly, approximately 3–6 hours. Sizing both sides will brace the board. If the board is cradled then the back does not need to be sized. Wash your brush thoroughly before it dries.

If, once painting, it is apparent that the sizing was insufficient (the paint is sinking), then a coat of acrylic picture varnish may be applied over the painting and allowed to dry. This will act as an acrylic retouch varnish. Use two coats or a stronger size for the next painting or try Lascaux acrylic size (see *List of sources*, page 165).

GROUNDS

A ground allows colour, absorbency and texture to be altered and controlled.

Acrylic is non-injurious to its support.

Acrylic paint is best applied to an acrylic ground. Each manufacturer produces a primer to go with their range, made of the same acrylic emulsion. The primer also contains white pigment, or white pigment and a coarse extender. The former is called acrylic primer, and the latter is called acrylic gesso primer. Acrylic gesso primer has more tooth from the coarse extender which is often chalk. The use of chalk has resulted in the term 'gesso' being adopted for such primers. N.B. In this book, the term 'gesso' is used to mean genuine gesso. The ground is simply an extended, stiff white acrylic paint.

Either primer will afford the paint the right degree of absorbency and flexibility. They are cheap and extremely quick and easy to apply.

Priming with tube colours is comparatively expensive but there is no structural disadvantage.

Other grounds

Oil and oil modified (alkyd) grounds are too greasy. The acrylic would probably peel off.

Gesso is acceptable for acrylic but the amount of preparation compared to acrylic primer makes it only worth using when its exact surface character is desired.

Gesso will need sizing if handling properties are required similar to using sized paper or acrylic-primed supports. There is no structural objection to unsized gesso but it will be an absorbent ground. For sizing gesso for acrylic, see page 46.

The presence of rabbit-skin glue in the gesso does not prevent the acrylic from adhering to it, because it is mixed with whiting.

APPLYING ACRYLIC GROUND

Apply acrylic ground at full strength.

Prime the edges of a support as well as the face. Prime both sides of an uncradled board to prevent uneven tension and warping. Apply an even number of layers to both sides; missing just one coat from the reverse can make the board warp.

A wavy mottler will produce a thin even coat similar to oil primer on canvas, and will give a thin coat on canvas in a similar way to oil primer (see page 26). However, as acrylic primer is easier to apply than oil primer a wavy mottler is not so indispensable; a decorator's brush is adequate. A plastic card (old phonecard/bankcard) can scrape a very thin layer on to a board but can leave ridges. A very smooth effect can be achieved by sanding the primer in between coats, using a medium (4/0–6/0) garnet paper. Garnet paper cuts better than glass paper.

When using a mottler on open canvas place a piece of card between the stretcher and canvas to prevent the stretcher bars showing (see fig. 23).

One coat is structurally adequate, but two or more coats will produce a whiter ground. Two coats with a mottler on canvas will not fill in the weave, if you want it filled apply 3 or 4 coats. For a very smooth acrylic ground, sand each dry coat of acrylic primer. Applying several coats does not reduce the flexibility of the ground as in oil priming. Wash your brush before the primer dries. Leave the primer to dry, approximately 15–60 minutes. Each successive coat will take longer to dry.

A litre of acrylic primer will cover a 137 × 168 cm (54 × 66″) canvas with four coats. See fig. 37.

The colour of the ground

If a transparent or partly transparent palette is to be used then the ground should be white so that the maximum amount of light is reflected back and the painting will appear and remain as bright as possible.

You can colour the dry white acrylic ground before painting with a transparent colour. Use at least three coats of primer to get as white a ground as possible. Dilute the chosen colour with approximately 50% water. Brush on and leave to dry. The light can still pass through this veil to the white ground.

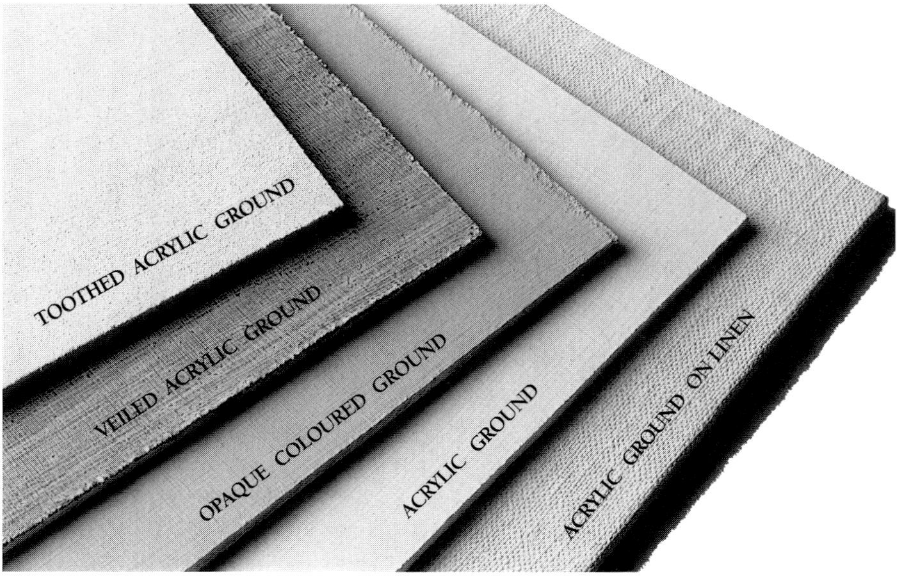

37. *Types of acrylic grounds.*

If an opaque palette is to be used then a white ground is not necessary. The light will not travel through the paint layer. The primer could be coloured with any colour you want. Mix the two together before applying. Tinting the primer with the colour you want is more economical than priming with paint. For some full strength colours this is not possible and paint will have to be used.

Adding tooth to acrylic primer

More tooth can be added to either a primer or a paint. This is done by adding an inert pigment (see page 98). These pigments are also noted in full in the pigment list (page 131). Mix the chosen pigment with a little primer until it is lump-free. Then mix this paste into the primer or paint. Keep the addition of pigment to approximately 10% so that the ground remains flexible. Mixing pigment directly into the primer will produce lumps and the extra pigment will not be dispersed and suspended in the binder. An even toothier ground can be made by using acrylic emulsion and approximately 30% inert pigment. See fig. 37.

Coloured and toothed ground

Acrylic grounds can be coloured and toothed by using a combination of both methods.

Final precaution for bracing uncradled boards

Apply a layer of paint on the reverse of the support to equalize the effect of any movement on the painting.

ACRYLIC PAINT

The binder

Acrylic emulsion is made from polymer resins. The most stable acrylic emulsion for artists' use is an acrylic co-polymer emulsion.

The pigment and the paint

The pigment must be evenly dispersed and suspended in acrylic emulsion (see fig. 32). In order to do this chemical adjustments are made to the paint and a percentage of extender is sometimes used.

See pigment chapter (page 127) for permanent pigments and *List of sources* (page 165) for brands of paint.

Making your own acrylic paint or primer

There is a substantial lack of recipes or information on this. Pigments do not disperse or suspend well in acrylic emulsion without the use of additives. It would seem unwise to make your own paint or primer without knowing how to produce a stable film.

Two manufacturers make aqueous dispersions, or colour pastes, to mix with acrylic emulsion. These are pigments which have already been suspended in water. See *List of sources*, page 165.

Manufactured acrylic colour versus colour pastes

These two types of acrylic paint inevitably offer different possibilities and are equally acceptable provided the colour paste is used in the manufacturer's recommended way, i.e. with the correct type and percentage of binder.

PVA colours

Cheaper ranges of paint are made using polyvinyl acetate as a binder instead of polymer resins and less expensive pigments which may be extended as well. They are inferior to acrylic paints in handling properties and permanence.

Resoluble acrylic paint

Acrylic paint can be made so it remains water-soluble once dry. See *List of sources*, page 165.

Thinners

The thinners for acrylic paint is water. If problems occur with pigments separating from the binder, i.e. looking granular or dusty, then use distilled water instead of tap water. Metals and salts in tap water can effect the binder in this manner. Distilled water is not just boiled water, it is produced by collecting the steam from boiling water. See *List of sources*, page 165. Dusting off can also occur if the paint is thinned excessively, thereby reducing the binder to almost nothing.

Mediums

With each brand of paint there are several different mediums sold. These are usually adaptations of the paint binder.

Mediums should be used according to manufacturer's instructions.

Retarding the drying rate of paint

Retarders are sold with each paint range and should be used according to manufacturer's instructions.

Sinking paint and retouch varnish

If you have any problems with acrylic paint sinking, paint on a thin layer of acrylic picture varnish as a retouch layer. This will act as a size and reduce the absorbency of the previous paint layer or support.

Brushes and palettes

Dried acrylic emulsion is more or less ruinous to brushes. Do not allow paint to dry on brushes – it only takes 10–15 minutes! Even when brushes are kept washed, dried acrylic emulsion can build up at the root of the brush after a while. Synthetic brushes may therefore be more economical for acrylic painting. If you need to remove dried paint then try soaking the brush in methylated spirit or acetone. See *List of sources*, page 165.

A piece of formica is a good palette because dry paint can be soaked off with water or scraped off. Glass is good too but it can be smashed.

Resuming a picture when the paint is dry

New acrylic paint will take over dry paint provided the old paint is washed clean first with a soft cloth and water containing a drop of washing-up liquid, followed by a rinse with plain water. There should not be a residue of water on the painting. Washing is not necessary if the painting is only a few weeks old.

CARE OF AN ACRYLIC PAINTING

Acrylic paintings absorb dirt, particularly in warm temperatures. Unfortunately, varnishes tend to be impractible to remove without damaging the paint film, even those made for acrylic paintings.

The only safe way to keep an acrylic painting clean is to keep it in a portfolio or a glazed frame. See *Appendix C* (page 160) for information on framing and hanging. A thin wax picture varnish can be applied to produce an even sheen.

Removing canvases from stretchers

Acrylic paintings are less delicate than oil paintings and can withstand rolling better. However, this should still be avoided because of the tediousness of re-stretching the painting, and rolling it certainly won't be good for it. Roll it with the picture on the outside around as large a diameter tube as possible. Any cracks will then fold in on themselves. An expandable stretcher will be necessary to stretch the canvas flat again.

Chapter 3
ENCAUSTIC PAINTING

Encaustic is painting with pigment bound in wax.

Encaustic means 'burning in' and refers to a wax painting being fused and driven into its ground or support by the use of heat.

Encaustic is extremely durable, can be transparent or opaque, used thinly or as an impasto/texturally, contains no extenders, can be matt or semi-gloss, can be used without a ground and is the only thick paint medium which can be resumed at any time and made wet or removed by the use of heat.

Gradation of layers

Encaustic paint has the same degree of strength and flexibility regardless of the pigment. There is therefore no need to consider which colours can go on top of one another. This relates to requirements in other media.

SUPPORTS

Encaustic is not destructive to its support.

Encaustic best grips a support which has a key and/or is absorbent. A ground is only necessary if you want to manipulate the colour, absorbency or texture of the support.

Canvas on open stretchers is not recommended for encaustic because the paint is not flexible enough to withstand the movement of the canvas. Canvas should be stretched on a cradled board if you want to paint on it.

Note: Because of the heat used in encaustic it is not possible to glue the canvas down, blisters will develop as the cloth comes away from the board. A cradled board should be used so canvas can be stretched over it and stapled at the back of the chassis. The canvas must be flat and tight as the encaustic paint will not tighten it. Make sure you keep the weave of the cloth parallel with the board. See gesso chapter for boards (page 85) and oil chapter for stretching canvas (page 14).

Types of cloth recommended are the same as for acrylic (see page 45), except if using gesso, see the types of canvas recommended for oil painting (page 11).

Boards such as MDF, hardboard and Sundeala are recommended as for gesso boards (see page 85).

The disadvantage of plywood, blockboard and chipboard remain as for gesso boards (see page 87).

Boards larger than 60 cm (24") square need to be mounted on a chassis (see page 87).

Boards should be degreased and sanded before a ground or paint is applied (see page 89).

Metals: Copper is a good support for encaustic because of its rigidity. It is far more expensive than wood-based boards. Plates should be degreased and sanded with coarse (P120) wet-and-dry paper (also waterproof silicon carbide paper). Steel is not good because it rusts and zinc discolours the paint.

Sculptural pieces: Encaustic is good for use on sculptural pieces because the paint structure is so simple and no varnish is necessary.

Paper is not recommended for encaustic because the paint film is not flexible enough to withstand the movement of the paper.

GROUNDS

A ground offers the manipulation of colour, absorbency or texture of the support.

Unsized gesso is a good absorbent ground. It can be white, coloured, textured, patterned, etc. See gesso chapter (page 85).

Oil and alkyd grounds are heat sensitive and would blister. They are also not absorbent enough for encaustic.

Acrylic grounds are heat sensitive and would blister and are not absorbent enough for encaustic.

ENCAUSTIC PAINT

Encaustic paint is sold in a very small range by one company in the UK. See *List of sources*, page 165. It is in fact the easiest paint to make and you can then ensure and control the quality of the binder and pigments yourself.

The binder

The binder is beeswax or a mixture of waxes. Beeswax is best because it does not yellow or embrittle over time. Natural beeswax is best because it is more flexible than bleached beeswax. Bleached beeswax (also called 'refined') reverts to yellow in time anyway. See photograph (fig. 44). Natural beeswax comes in pellets or lumps, although lump seems less available nowadays.

Carnauba wax is used to produce a harder paint and to make it less heat sensitive. Carnauba wax is scraped from the leaves of a Brazilian palm tree. The yellow type is from the young leaves whilst the grey is from the old leaves. Refined carnauba is filtered grey wax. See photograph (fig. 44). The yellow type is best for encaustic because of its pale colour.

The melting point of the binder is raised by using part carnauba. The melting point of the paint can be important if you don't want the underneath paint to melt and lift off when you apply more hot paint.

Beeswax must not be burnt. It will turn brown which will mask the colour of the paint and reduce its flexibility. The fumes from burning wax are poisonous and hot wax is a fire hazard. A double boiler should be used to avoid any of the above. You might like to keep a top part of a boiler exclusively for melting wax. This will save you having to scrupulously clean it for other uses.

A total of 500 g (18 oz) of binder will make approximately six small pots of paint.

Take 425 g (15 oz) of beeswax and 75 g (3 oz) of carnauba wax, i.e. 85% beeswax to 15% carnauba. Melt it in the top part of a double boiler for 5–10 minutes. Watch it to make sure the wax doesn't burn and the water doesn't boil away nor splash into the binder.

38. *Natural beeswax lump and pellets.*

39. *Microcrystalline wax.*

40. *Natural yellow carnauba flakes and lump.*

If a softer paint is wanted then replace the carnauba with microcrystalline wax. Microcrystalline wax is also less sensitive to heat than beeswax. You can also mix all three waxes. Keep the proportion of beeswax at approximately 70% as it is the most durable component.

See *Other encaustic binders*, page 59.

PIGMENTS

Any permanent pigment should be used. See pigment chapter, page 127. Choose pigments according to whether you want a transparent or opaque or mixed palette. Transparency of the paint will not equal oil paint because the wax is far more opaque than oil.

The most toxic pigments should be avoided in their dry form, e.g. flake white, and a respirator with the correct filter on it should be used when handling dry pigments. Flake white has no advantages over titanium or zinc in encaustic. See pigment list (page 131) and *Health and safety* (page 9).

MAKING THE PAINT

The paint is made with the molten binder. It is made and kept on a hot plate because the binder sets in minutes when it is removed from the heat.

The hot plate

This can be a domestic hot tray or a photographic hot plate. If using a domestic hot tray do not reuse it for food. Equipment should not pass between kitchen and studio.

An improvised hot plate is a metal plate over an electric ring. A double ring gives a good size palette. Iron, stainless steel or aluminium are fine, galvanised steel or zinc are not because they discolour the paints. The sheet should be at least 6 mm ($\frac{1}{4}''$) thick and 50 mm (2″) bigger than the top of the heat source in each direction. Suspend the plate 50 mm (2″) above the heat by standing it on bricks or by welding sides on it, this keeps the whole palette at a more even temperature.

a.  b. 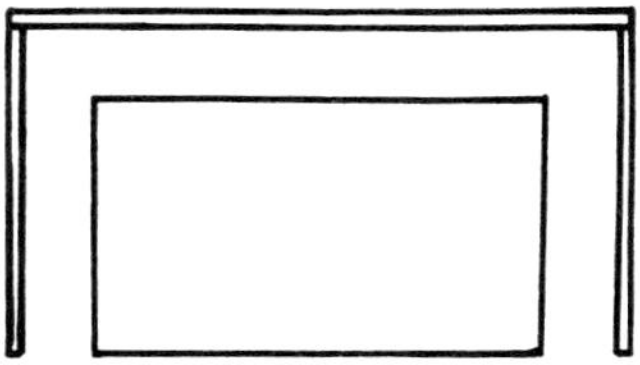

41. *Metal plate suspended above electric ring:* a. *supported on bricks, and* b. *with metal sides.*

Paint the underside of the metal with a matt black paint. This helps the metal to absorb the heat.

Whichever hot plate is used, make sure the paint is not burnt, i.e. control the heat setting!

Mixing the colours

Empty, clean food tins are good containers. Glass is okay but likely to break.

With the empty tins on the hot plate fill each one with molten binder.

Then stir in the pigments well with a palette knife. You can use up to 40% pigment in each colour. The binder cannot hold more than that. The colour will however be very powerful with much less than 40% pigment. Using less pigment will give a more transparent colour, even with an opaque pigment. There is no minimum amount structurally required, you can make it as you like it.

Keep the tins of colour on the hot plate or they will set.

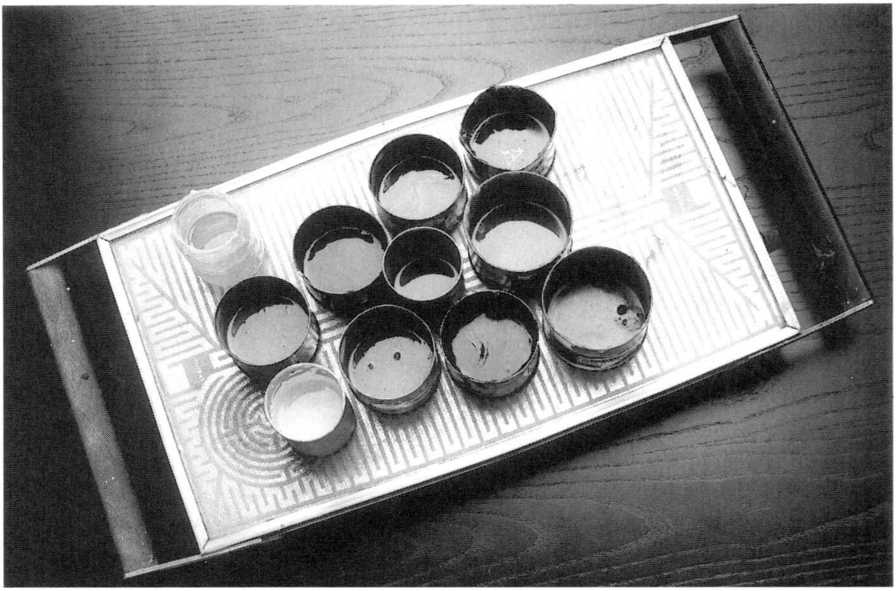

42. *Tins of paint and binder on hot plate.*

Stir the paint before and during use to ensure the pigment is thoroughly suspended in the hot wax. If you experience any problems of pigment separation from the binder, you can mull one colour at a time on the hot plate.

Thinners

There are no thinners for encaustic paint except for the binder itself. Keep a tin of this on the hot plate to thin the colours out, i.e. you can make a tin of reasonably pigmented colour and then reduce it for transparency on the palette without having to make an extra tin of more transparent colour.

There is only one basic consistency of paint in encaustic.

White spirit should not be used to thin hot paint because of the fire risk. White spirit in the paint can also cause separation of pigment and binder.

Mediums

The binder is the thinners and medium. You could use any binder as a thinner regardless of which one you made the paints with.

See *Other encaustic binders* (page 59) for other recipes and information.

Brushes

The paint itself will not do any harm to your brushes. But you may find it practical to keep a brush for each colour. As the paint congeals at room temperature the brush becomes a hard lump of paint. The easiest thing to do is to leave it and re-melt the paint when you want that colour. This can be at any time (years afterwards!) because the paint does not dry or attract dirt like oil and acrylic, i.e. you consign brushes to encaustic. So it might be more economical to use synthetic brushes. If you want to clean a brush, then melt (holding brush down on hot palette) and wipe all the paint off with a rag and then wash it with white spirit followed by soap and water. Do not use the white spirit near the hot plate as there is a fire risk.

HOW TO COPE WITH ENCAUSTIC

Encaustic requires changes in habit because the paint is only wet when it's hot.

Brushes can be stood in an empty tin on the hot plate to keep them from setting hard. Stand them up around the edge so the colours stay clean. When you have finished for the day, take them out of the tin, shape them with a rag and lay flat so they set with the hairs straight.

To paint, either pour colours out on to the hot plate or straight on to the support, or use clean spoons/palette knives to remove paint from each tin. Otherwise colours will contaminate each other. Don't leave utensils in the tins whilst the paint sets because you won't be able to pull them out!

Any heated tools can be used provided they don't burn the waxes, e.g. irons, soldering irons. Heated palette knives may be available, particularly in the USA.

The palette can be cleaned by wiping with a rag whilst it is still hot.

Because the paint cools as soon as you take the brush off the heat, a thick layer of paint will be laid down on the support. Thin layers are obtained by using a hair dryer or infra-red lamp (a type of light bulb which emits heat) to heat the paint on the support. A hot-air gun is too hot and can burn you, but one with a variable heat setting is usable.

At the end of each painting session simply turn off the hot plate. When resuming, turn the hot plate on approximately thirty minutes in advance in order to melt the tins of colour. Any colours out on the hot plate will melt again too. The tins do not need lids, any dust on the hard surface can be wiped off before melting the paint.

Unique to encaustic, you can resume the painting at any time, even years afterwards. Layers of paint grip each other by the burning in process (see page 58); you won't find old paint resisting new. The painting can be melted at any time for you to paint wet into wet or wipe off entirely.

Encaustic paint can be used cold as wax pastels. A very thin layer of paint can be rubbed on the support with cold paint. Oil pastels and scraping techniques can also be used with encaustic. See pages 110 and 119 for full explanation. Some coloured pencils will also melt with heat.

BURNING IN

This is an expression, the paint is not literally 'burned'.

When you have finished your painting the layers of paint are fused together and driven into the ground/support by the application of heat. The paint film will grip the ground/support.

Lay the painting flat and hold the infra-red lamp approximately 30 cm (12") above it. Move the lamp over the painting as the paint melts. If you over-melt, underlaying colours will seep through the top ones. It won't harm the painting if you want to do this. Lightweight pigments particularly will float to the surface whilst heavyweight pigments will sink, i.e. ivory black will rise up through cadmium red.

43. *Burning in.*

Painting can be resumed even after burning in. You can burn in at intermediary stages if you want; the main point is that you do it when the painting is finished for long term stability.

Final precaution for bracing uncradled boards and copper plates

Apply a layer of paint on the reverse of the support to equalize the effect of movement on the painting.

FINISH AND CARE OF AN ENCAUSTIC PAINTING

After heat treatment the painting will be matt. A gloss/semi-gloss is obtained by polishing the painting. Use a soft cloth and buff the painting or the parts of the painting you want to be glossy.

Encaustic paint does not attract dust. It does not need varnishing nor a glazed frame. It can be dusted when dirty.

Use your common sense however and keep encaustic paintings in those conditions which you would afford to any work of art. See *Appendix C*, page 160.

OTHER ENCAUSTIC BINDERS

The following notes give information on other binders which you may want to use or experiment with. Take heed of the information given if you are going to experiment, e.g. with oils in a binder (see page 60).

The pure beeswax binder gives a very soft paint which is very heat sensitive. It is therefore more susceptible to damage by scuffing and lifting off with subsequent hot paint. Pure beeswax may be more useful when intending to use the paint cold, i.e. as wax pastels. See *Drawing materials*, page 119.

The reduction in flexibility of bleached beeswax is not enough to ban its use. If you have some, use it up before you buy unbleached, or better still, use it up in bits by substituting some bleached for part of the natural beeswax.

44. *Clockwise: Bleached lump beeswax; damar resin; grey carnauba wax; bleached beeswax pellets; refined beeswax* (centre).

Grey carnauba wax is not recommended because it is so dark. Refined carnauba is more acceptable though not readily available to artists.

Damar resin (also incorrectly called gum damar) will raise the melting point of the binder and produce a harder paint, similar to carnauba, but will eventually yellow and is more brittle than carnauba.

Paraffin waxes are not recommended because they yellow and embrittle in the course of time.

Using oil is not generally recommended, principally because the oil dries and prevents the making of paints which can be melted and used indefinitely. It also prevents unlimited re-working of a painting. Two of the unique characteristics of encaustic which are too good to give up! The oil will also increase yellowing. It is debatable whether wax paint containing oil should be termed encaustic.

See page 171 and *Impasto* (page 33) for using beeswax in oil paint.

Chapter 4
TEMPERA PAINTING

Tempera is a paint which uses an emulsion as its vehicle. An emulsion is a stable mixture of an aqueous solution with an oily one (oil, wax or resin). Incidentally, this also includes acrylic paint.

There are many tempera recipes, all ultimately offering their own characteristics. See *Other tempera recipes* and notes (page 71).

However, this chapter is going to discuss two natural temperas, egg and gum, chosen because they use the simplest methods and because they display best those characteristics which are only possible with tempera. They give the added advantage of a greater choice of colours than the small ranges of manufactured egg/oil paints.

Character of tempera paint

Tempera made from natural emulsions is luminous, matt and at its most glowing when used translucently. Opaque layers tend to approximate gouache which is much easier to use for the same effect! It dries quickly to a partly insoluble film, becoming quite insoluble after some months. Its glowing skin-like appearance is obtained by many superimposed layers of paint. It cannot be moved around on the support like the other media. Subsequent painting can only be resumed within a certain period of time.

Its strength is the unique appearance of the colours.

SUPPORTS

Tempera is not flexible enough to be used on canvas or paper and must be used on boards. See gesso chapter (page 85). Gesso on canvas which is mounted on board is structurally more acceptable than open stretched canvas but the glowing nature of the paint will be reduced by the weave of the canvas.

Tempera cannot be used on a board without gesso because the board does not offer the right absorbency or colour.

GROUNDS

Gesso is used as the ground for tempera painting because it has the right degree of absorbency which can be readily adjusted for this type of paint to grip the ground. See gesso chapter (page 94). It is also white.

Acrylic, oil and alkyd grounds are not absorbent enough for tempera.

Coloured grounds

See gesso chapter (page 95).

TEMPERA PAINT

There are only three brands of tempera on the market which are all egg/oil emulsions. These are useful if you are going into tempera painting in a small way and are less likely to produce a good standard of paint, or if you want to use tempera to paint into wet oil paint. See *Appendix A* (page 145) for brand details and *Using tempera over wet oil paint* (page 70). In order to use egg or gum tempera you have to make your own.

Egg tempera

Egg tempera is the best known natural tempera. It is used thinly. Egg tempera does not offer any impasto effects. Any thick layers tend to move before they dry and a thick layer will not adhere well to the gesso – it may peel or crack.

The binder is chicken egg yolk. The yolk is an emulsion of egg oil particles suspended in albumen (aqueous solution). The eggs should be as fresh as possible; the paint will last longer and the paint film will be more durable.

Gum tempera

Gum tempera offers minimal impasto effects as well as thin painting. It is slower drying than egg tempera, less transparent and blends more easily.

The binder is an emulsion of stand oil, damar varnish and glycerine (oily) suspended in gum kordofan (aqueous solution). Gum kordofan is more flexible and less soluble than other acacia gums. For explanation of gum kordofan, see page 81.

PIGMENTS

Any permanent pigment can be used. See pigment chapter, page 127.

Because pigments are used in their dry form to make the paint, the most toxic ones should be avoided particularly if making paint often. A respirator should be worn when handling dry pigments. See *Toxicity* (page 129) and *Health and safety* (page 9). Where a pigment is both toxic and sensitive to atmospheric pollution it would be doubly unwise to use it in tempera as the binder does not offer adequate protection against pollution.

Remember that opaque pigments appear more transparent because tempera is so thin.

Pigments may of course be mixed dry or as water pastes to obtain different colours or shades as well as mixing at the paint stage.

White in tempera

Flake white should be avoided because of its toxicity in dry form. Titanium tends to brush out better than zinc.

Distilled water

Only distilled water is used in tempera painting. Metals and salts in tap water can separate the pigments from the binder, leaving dusty pigment particles exposed on top of the gesso. 'Water' should be read as 'distilled water' throughout this chapter. Distilled water is not just boiled water, it is produced by collecting the steam from boiling water.

The paint

Tempera will not keep in tubes without preservatives, humidifiers and possibly stabilizers. This makes recipes more complicated and consequently more likely to go wrong. Vinegar is often recommended for egg but can interfere with its binding strength and can affect some colours adversely. It is simpler if the paint is made as it is needed, thereby removing the need for any of the above.

Pigments must be mulled in order to be wetted, dispersed and suspended in binder to produce a stable paint film. This is achieved by the friction between the surfaced muller and slab with the pigment paste in between. Mixing dry pigment and binder with a palette knife does not mull it and a weak film will be produced, often with dusty pigment deposits left on the gesso. The most efficient way of making tempera is in two stages:

i. The pigment is mulled in water and stored in paste form indefinitely.
ii. The binder is added as and when paint is required.
- *(a)* Egg tempera.
- *(b)* Gum tempera.

45. *Glass plate (slab) with sand-blasted surface, at least 46 cm (18") square, and* left to right: *paint scraper, palette knife; and muller.*

i. Mulling the pigment

Place a pile of pigment on the plate, make a well in the centre and pour in some water. Mix this to a rough paste with a palette knife adding more water if needed.

46. *Pigment and water.*

47. *Mixed paste.*

Some pigments do not wet easily. They can be persuaded by using some industrial methylated spirits with the water. (Ordinary methylated spirits may have to be used.) This will evaporate off and not interfere with the paint. See *List of sources*, page 165.

Once roughly mixed, mull the pigment until it is a smooth, creamy paste, i.e. move the muller across the plate, rubbing the pigment paste.

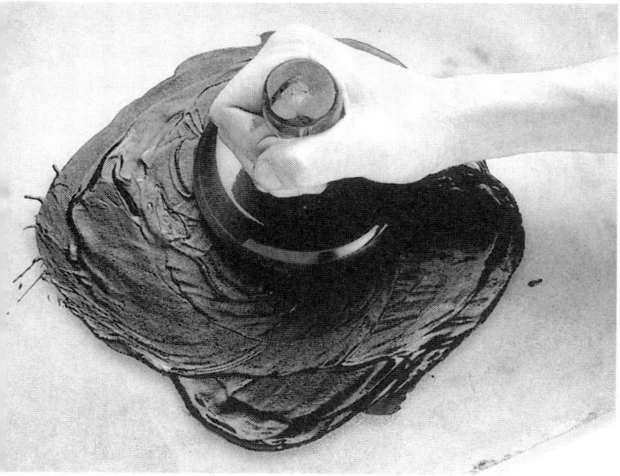

48. *Mulling pigment.*

49. *Gathering paste into middle of plate (slab).*

Periodically stop and scrape the paste back into the middle of the slab and off the muller, using the large palette knife or paint scraper.

Some pigments are initially very gritty; just keep working it!

This pigment paste will mix with the binder to produce a properly dispersed paint.

The paste can be kept in a lidded jar indefinitely. If it begins to dry out pour a little distilled water on top. If it dries out completely it can be re-mulled with water and put back in the jar.

The pastes could be kept in tubes if preferred. See page 42 for filling tubes.

50. *Mulled pigment. Also see fig. 32.*

Upkeep of muller and plate (slab)

See *Appendix B* (page 159) for cleaning muller and plate.

As the muller and plate are used, the sand-blasted surface of the glass is worn away. When it is smooth, mulling will take longer because of reduced friction. The surface of the muller and plate can be re-cut by mulling with a teaspoon of pink-fused alumina and water, for approximately three minutes. Wash if off thoroughly with water. See *List of sources* (page 165) for pink-fused alumina. Other abrasives, e.g. carborundum, are less effective at re-cutting a surface in the glass.

ii.(a) The binder for egg tempera

When ready to paint, crack an egg and separate the yolk from the white. You can do this by tipping the yolk back and forth between two cups and letting the white fall out (fig. 51). The white is not used at all in the paint.

Once most of the white is gone, tip the yolk on to a piece of kitchen towel and roll it around. Any remaining white will come off. This will enable you to pick up the yolk between your thumb and forefinger (fig. 52).

Pierce the yolk sac with a point over a clean jar and the yolk will flow out. Discard the empty sac.

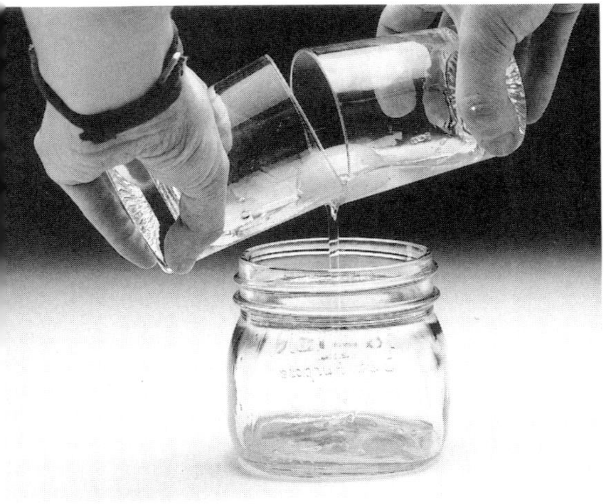

51. *Separating yolk and white.*

52. *Picking up the yolk.*

The colour of the yolk does not affect the paint because it bleaches out of the paint quickly.

ii.(b) The binder for gum tempera

The binder is made of the following ingredients:

5 parts gum solution*
1 part stand oil mixed with 1 part damar varnish**
$\frac{3}{4}$ part glycerine

***Gum solution:** Measure 56 g (2 oz) of kordofan gum and crush it wrapped in a rag with a hammer. Pour 142 ml (5 fl oz) of hot water over it and leave it to dissolve, between 3–12 hours. Strain the solution through a tea strainer to remove bits of bark.

****Making damar varnish:** It is cheaper to make varnish than to buy it.

Choose the pieces of damar resin with the least colour and dirt. Tie 170 g (6 oz) of damar resin (see fig. 44) into a muslin bag and suspend it in a jar of 284 ml (10 fl.oz) of turpentine. Turpentine is a more thorough solvent for damar than white spirit. This produces a varnish of similar strength to the shop bought ones.

Keep the lid on the jar to prevent turpentine evaporating. The resin will dissolve in 12–24 hours.

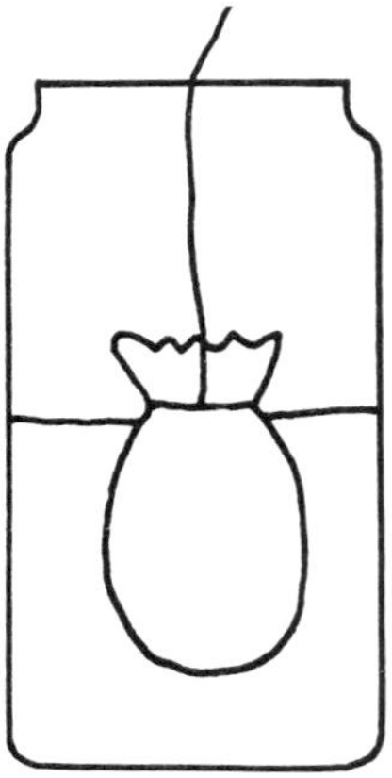

53. *Damar bag in turpentine.*

Resist the temptation of dispensing with the muslin bag. It can take up to a year for the resin to dissolve if it's at the bottom of the jar!

Damar varnish should be used up whilst fresh because of the turpentine content. For full information on turpentine, see page 31.

Stand oil is used rather than any other linseed oil because of its flexibility and non-yellowing features.

Although the gum solution would normally decompose, the binder can be kept for up to a year if retained in a sterilized jar which is full and sealed. A jar can be sterilized by filling it with boiling water (distilled not necessary). Let the water run over the top of the jar to ensure all the glass is sterilized. Mind your fingers! Alternatively, a proprietary sterilizing solution can be used. See *List of sources*, page 165. Glycerine has a preserving effect but you may wish to exclude it from the recipe. See *How to use tempera*, page 69.

Make sure the binder is fresh before use. If it is not, make a new batch. It will be watery and very smelly if it's gone off!

54. Left to right:
Gum solution, gum kordofan, glycerine.

55. *Whisking binder.*

Using a hand egg whisk or electric food mixture add the stand oil/damar mixture to the gum solution in a slow stream, mixing all the time. Continue mixing until a thick, white, homogenous liquid is produced, approximately five minutes.

Add the glycerine last and mix well. Glycerine improves brushability of the paint but increases solubility.

Mixing the paint

Mix equal parts (by volume) of pigment paste with binder to make the paint. This can be done on the palette with a brush or if you are using a lot of paint then you could put a yolk or an amount of gum in a cup and mix an equal volume of pigment paste with it using a palette knife.

Ensuring stability

Test each colour to ascertain stability and which pigments may need a different amount of binder (e.g. blues may need a little more).

Brush out each colour on clear glass and allow to dry thoroughly, approximately 12 hours. Using a flexible razor blade, see if each paint film can be peeled off without splintering. The colours which splinter require more binder.

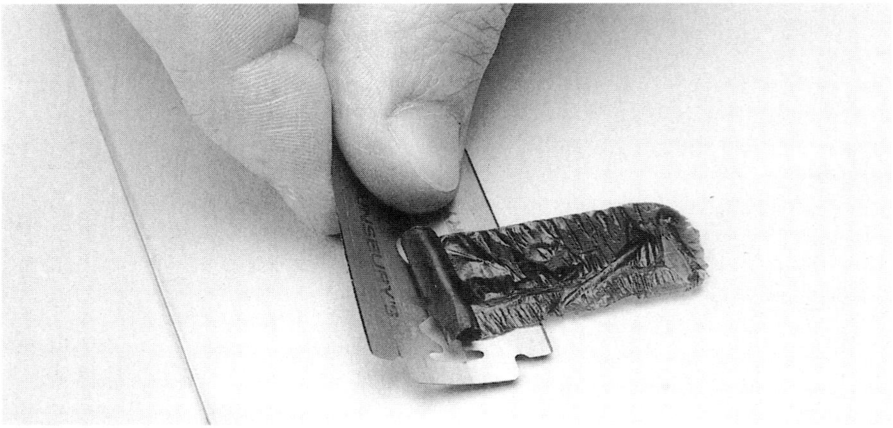

56. *Paint film peeled off glass.*

Too much binder will cause the paint to crack whilst too little will leave the pigment dry and underbound on the gesso. If the paint shows hair-line cracks, reduce the amount of binder/increase the amount of water.

Remember that in the actual painting, the absorbency of the gesso and the amount of thinners used will affect the paint film and must be controlled.

Gradation of layers rule

If it is noticeably only the top layer of paint which has cracked then it may be that the top layer has more binder in it than the previous layer. The stronger paint layer contracts and cracks. If such a problem arises, add more water to successive layers of paint.

Absorbency of gesso

An underbound paint may also be produced by too absorbent a gesso. Having tested your paint as above and reduced the amount of thinners used, if the paint is still becoming dusty, then the gesso is probably too absorbent. The gesso can be sized to control its absorbency (see page 94).

Quality of tempera paint film

In order to produce a durable tempera painting you must strive to ensure the pigment is not left underbound. In total you must control the absorbency of the gesso, amount of binder in each colour and the amount of thinners used.

Storing the paint

Egg tempera will last approximately 2–3 days if kept in a cool, dark place. After that time the egg will start to decompose. Not only does this stink but it obviously starts to destroy the binding properties of the egg.

The paint can last up to a week in the fridge, but the cold may affect the colour of some pigments.

Gum tempera will decompose in a similar manner because the paint cannot be kept in sterile conditions.

If you keep the paint for a few days make sure you keep it at its original consistency by adding water as the paint thickens. Do not use any surface skin as paint. If you have the paint in cups during painting then a damp rag or damp sheet of blotting paper can double as a humidifier and cover.

USING THE PAINT

Thinners

Distilled water is the only thinners for tempera. Before use, the paint is thinned with water, just enough to enable it to be brushed out. The paint should not be viscous, particularly egg tempera. Too thick a layer of egg tempera will crack, but too much water will produce an underbound paint film.

There is only one basic consistency of paint in tempera.

Medium

There is no medium for tempera other than distilled water.

How to use tempera

A tempera painting is made by the superimposition of paint layers.

The most important part of tempera painting is not to paint in a back and forth motion as is the habit in all other media. This muddies the paint on the gesso. Lay the colour on by one brushstroke only, lift the brush and wait for the paint to dry before the next layer. This takes only a minute.

In order to build up optimum translucency the amount of paint on the brush also needs to be controlled. A full brush will deposit thick edges and a blob at the end of the stroke. This will show through to the next layer and the translucency will be reduced. Wiping the brush on a rag between the palette and the painting will remove excess paint and result in an even brushstroke being made.

Even when dry, the tempera is susceptible to being lifted or muddied by the subsequent layer. Gum tempera is particularly re-soluble. The painting cannot be built up if the underneath layers are constantly being picked up or muddied. Excluding glycerine from the gum tempera will reduce solubility. However, a complete absence may make it difficult to brush the paint out. Painters should adjust the recipe according to their needs.

Colours cannot be mixed on the gesso board. They have to be mixed on the palette or laid, wet on dry, on top of one another on the gesso.

The painting can be resumed up to approximately eight months after the last layer was applied. After that the new paint does not seem to join with the previous layers but rather floats on top.

Using tempera over wet oil paint

Tempera can be used over wet/tacky oil paint for crisp textural and visual effects, unlike those made by painting wet into wet with oil paint. A blob or line of tempera does not merge with oil paint, thus producing the crisp effect. The tempera cannot be worked on the canvas, you can only lay the paint on and leave it, or completely remove it again.

This method of painting can be difficult as the tempera layer is apt to crack the wider the stroke is, or if the oil layer is too wet or too thick, or if the tempera dries too quickly. Use this method only when you occasionally need the crisp effect.

An egg/oil tempera is recommended for maximum adhesion of the two media, particularly if the tempera is subsequently covered by more oil paint, e.g. glazing the tempera with oil paint. See following egg/oil recipe and/or *Appendix A* (page 148) for brands of paint.

If you are going to overpaint with oil then you need to wait until the original oil layer is dry or the tempera may be picked up as the brush moves the original oil layer. If the tempera itself tends to be soluble when further oil paint is applied, try using a binder without damar in it (damar remains soluble in turpentine, although it should be somewhat protected by the stand oil and egg), e.g.:

1 part stand oil
1 part turpentine
2 parts whole beaten egg (see egg/oil recipe, page 71)
2 parts distilled water

CARE OF A TEMPERA PAINTING

Protection

Tempera paintings need protection from pollution similar to oil paintings (see page 38).

Drying time

A tempera painting is surface-dry within hours. However, the longer the painting is left (up to about a year) the harder, less absorbent and more insoluble the paint film becomes.

Glazed frames

A tempera painting can be given a satiny gloss by polishing/buffing it with a soft cloth – silk is good. Buffing should only be done after the paint has hardened. The painting can be kept clean in a glazed frame.

If your painting is in any way dusty or fragile when buffed, this indicates a faulty paint film. Try to identify your faults and correct them for the next painting. See *Ensuring stability*, page 68.

A fragile tempera painting must be kept under glass because a varnish would not be removable without taking some of the paint with it. A thin wax picture varnish can be applied to produce an even sheen.

Varnishing

An absorbent or weak paint film will allow the varnish to sink into the painting, making it very difficult to remove without damaging the painting. Varnishing should only be done once the paint has thoroughly dried and hardened and if the paint film is sound. Buffing the surface may also make it less absorbent.

Varnish as for oil painting (see page 39).

OTHER TEMPERA RECIPES, including notes

Egg emulsion

Whole egg does not cause any structural problem in a binder but the resultant paint is more awkward than an egg-yolk binder as it dries very quickly and is more difficult to brush out.

Egg/Oil emulsion

An egg/oil emulsion gives results tending towards a gum emulsion but to a lesser extent. Egg/oil recipes are morely like to go wrong than gum tempera. They can produce paint which cracks or won't dry. Its best use is for overpainting into wet oil paint (see page 70). A reliable recipe is:

Mix together:
- 2 parts whole beaten egg
- 2 parts distilled water

Strain through a tea strainer to remove the yolk sac and clots.

Mix together:
- 1 part stand oil
- 1 part damar varnish

Combine the two mixtures with a beater until they emulsify.

The damar varnish is desirable because the turpentine in it helps the whole mixture emulsify and the damar seems to have a preserving effect on the binder. The stand oil is better than other linseed oils because of its flexibility and non-yellowing features. Defects in egg/oil emulsions seem less likely to occur when the whole egg is used rather than just the yolk.

There are plenty of recipes in other books for various egg/oil emulsions but be careful as it's easy to go wrong! See following note.

Other possible emulsions

Egg/oil emulsions can also be made so that they are soluble in turps instead of water.

Beeswax emulsions offer similar effects to gum tempera.

Drying oils should not be combined with wax emulsions because the resulting binder would yellow badly.

Wax/glue and wax/casein emulsions are recommended instead.

Casein and drying oil emulsions are not recommended as they turn yellow/brown.

Glue/oil and egg/gum emulsions are also possible.

See other chapters, via *Index*, for photographs of ingredients.

Note: Although all these binders and their variations are each ultimately unique, there is a common lack of tested recipes and information on them. There is enormous scope for research and documentation on temperas. Artists need to know which binders offer alternative effects and which are stable.

Perhaps artists themselves will turn to the arduous task of experimenting and documenting with alternative binders for problem pigments or when searching for a specific effect.

See *Bibiography* (page 172).

Chapter 5
WATERCOLOUR AND GOUACHE PAINTING

Watercolour is transparent, matt, re-soluble, and used thinly. When resuming a watercolour it cannot be to start again but to add, the stains in the paper will show through all the subsequent layers.

Gouache is opaque watercolour. It is also matt and re-soluble. When resuming a gouache, a residue will still mark the paper but the new layer of paint will mask it because of its opacity.

It is used more thickly than watercolour but it is the combined mattness and opacity which produces the body effect of the paint.

Gradation of layers

Watercolour and gouache colours are approximately equal in strength and can therefore be applied on top of each other in any order. This relates to requirements in other media.

SUPPORTS AND GROUNDS

Watercolour and gouache paint are not destructive to their support and therefore do not need a ground. Paper offers watercolour and gouache just the right grip. Paper is both the support and ground. Rag paper is recommended (see page 102).

A painting will appear brighter if it is executed on a Rough or Not sheet as opposed to an HP (hot-pressed) sheet. Rough and Not surfaces have a greater surface area resulting in more pigment particles being deposited and more colour reflected back through them.

For explanation of paper surfaces, see page 106.

57. *Cross-sections of paper showing greater surface area of Rough and Not papers.*

Watercolour

The paper should be white so that the maximum amount of light is reflected back and the painting appears and remains as bright as possible. There is no structural objection to painting on coloured paper if you want the duller effects. See *Coloured paper* and *Colouring papers* (pages 115, 116).

Gouache

Because gouache is opaque, it is not necessary for the ground to be white. The light will not travel through the paint layer. The brightness of the paint comes only from the reflection of light through the pigment itself. Coloured papers can be used without affecting the stability of colour in the painting. Lightfast papers should be used if the paper is to be left exposed. See *Coloured paper* and *Colouring papers*, pages 115, 116.

Other supports and grounds

Canvas is not suitable for watercolour and gouache because the paint films cannot withstand canvas movement. Boards are not suitable as they do not offer a suitable grip. Neither are white enough for watercolour.

The amount of preparation time for the following two grounds makes their use impractical except when their exact surface characteristics are required.

Acrylic primer is too flexible for watercolour or gouache unless it is used on a board, or on canvas on board. For preparation, see page 47.

Gesso on board is suitable. It should be sized if you want a similar degree of control to watercolour or gouache on paper. Using gesso without size is structurally acceptable but the gesso can be rather absorbent. See gesso chapter for preparation of board and sizing (page 94).

Designers may use gouache on various supports for model making. However, if the model is to be kept as a work of art, then either paper and gouache should be used or a medium more suited to unusual supports. See *Bibliography* (page 17).

Preparation of paper

A heavyweight (400–600 gsm) paper will need no preparation provided the painting is executed with a moderate amount of water. If any excess of water is used or several layers are applied in quick succession the paper will need to be restrained (stretched) or it will cockle. Lightweight papers (approximately 185 gsm) will also need restraining. Cockling paper reduces the ways you can work and makes the picture awkward to keep or frame and can be off-putting visually.

Some watercolour paper is sold in blocks, as an attempt to keep the paper from cockling. These blocks are simply sheets of paper glued together around the edges, leaving a gap unglued so you can peel the top sheet off. Any water-rich or sustained painting will still cause cockling. A watercolour board is rag paper stuck to a board. these are relatively expensive and are probably the nearest to stretched paper. The quality of the board and glue is important as they should be acid-free and non-yellowing. Specific enquiry should be made to the manufacturer.

Stretching paper takes only about 15 minutes and presents a surface which stays flat regardless of the amount of water, length of time it is worked on or weight of sheet. It also allows you to save a lot of money by using lightweight paper.

Paper from any size up to approximately 150 × 250 m (59 × 98″) can be stretched. The tension built up in bigger sizes tends to split the paper.

There are two ways of stretching paper: *i.* on a flat board; *ii.* on a flat open frame.

A flat board gives a hard paper surface to paint on whilst the open frame gives a more sensitive, springy surface.

Painting area

The painting area is inside the gumstrip in *i*, and inside the chassis in *ii*. In *i* the gumstrip would show through the painting and is not acid-free and in *ii* it is too difficult to remove the glued border intact. See fig. 67.

i. On a flat board

The best drawing boards are those made of spruce wood. These stopped being made for artists about 30 years ago. One-sided wooden boards for draughtsmen are also spruce. Spruce withstands hundreds of cuts from a Stanley knife when cutting the paper off. Spruce-veneered boards were made and sold in art shops until recently but were very expensive.

58. *Spruce boards.*

If you are not lucky enough to have a spruce board then a man-made one stretches the paper just as well; it just wears out more quickly. Chipboard is the cheapest but if you find it too heavy then Sundeala is lighter. Use at least a 12 mm ($\frac{1}{2}$″) board. Thinner ones cannot withstand the tension of the stretched paper and will buckle. Hardboard is useless! If you are stretching on a 244 × 122 cm (8 × 4′) board then use as thick a board as possible, e.g. 38 mm ($1\frac{1}{2}$″) chipboard. Alternatively, you could brace a thinner board with a frame (see page 87) but this will mean only one side is available for stretching.

Preparation of new boards

Spruce boards need no preparation but man-made boards are initially too absorbent. The glue sinks into the board instead of sticking down the paper.

They can be sized with dilute shellac. Sizing is only repeated when you get a new board.

Measure 28 g (1 oz) of resin and 142 ml (5 fl.oz) of methylated spirits. Leave in a lidded jar to dissolve, between 12–24 hours. Alternatively, you can buy French polish and dilute it with approximately 40% methylated spirit. See *List of sources* (page 165).

Paint on to both sides of the board. Leave to dry for approximately 20 minutes.

59. *Orange shellac resin.*

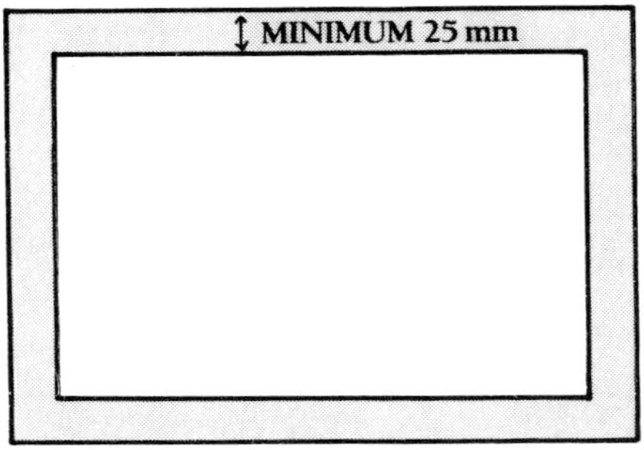

60. *Paper on board showing space for gumstrip.*

Paper preparation

Paper expands when soaked in water.

The paper is restrained by sticking it down by the edges whilst in an expanded state. Further application of water will not then cockle the paper.

Cut your paper to size. Make it at least 25 mm (1″) smaller than the board all the way round (fig. 60).

Submerge the paper either flat or rolled into a sink or bath of water. A heavy paper (600 gsm) will need approximately 15 minutes, whilst a lighter weight paper (185 gsm) needs only approximately 4 minutes.

If a sink or bath is not available the paper can be soaked by sponging (fig. 61). This method needs approximately 15–25 minutes on either side of the paper. Be careful not to rub the paper vigorously with the sponge because it will come off in little rolls and will looked skinned when dry. If you are very rough you can make holes in it (fig. 62).

Under soaking is one of the principle causes of failure in stretching paper. A sheet which is taped down when not fully expanded will not stretch flat or will cockle when painted on.

If using surface-sized paper (see page 104) then use cold water and don't over soak. Otherwise the glue may dissolve into the water.

61. *Paper soaking on board.*

62. *Wet paper disintegrating from rubbing.*

Gumstrip is used to tape down the expanded sheet. It can be washed off the board with water afterwards.

Keep your hands dry when touching the gumstrip roll. Any water across the diameter of the roll will stick the whole roll together. Cut the gumstrip to length with dry hands whilst the paper is soaking.

Once soaked, drain the paper. Either sponge off the excess or if the paper is strong enough and not too large hold it vertically over the sink. A piece of Formica mounted vertically over the sink is excellent for draining (see fig. 64). The wet paper will cling on to it and the water will run off. A clean, tiled wall in a bathroom can also be used.

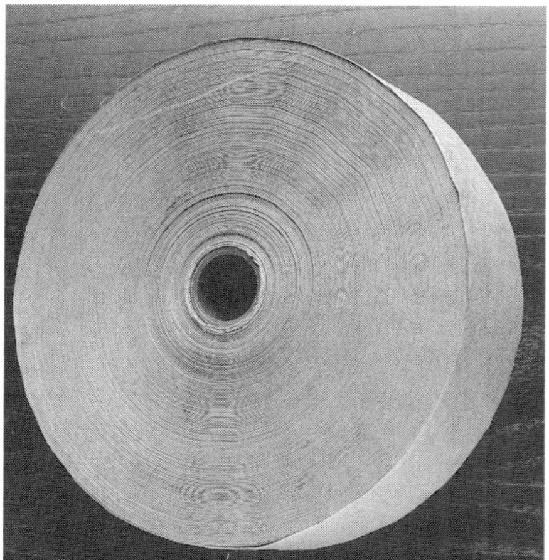

63. *Gumstrip.*

64. *Paper draining on Formica over sink.*

Lay the paper flat on the board. Pat out any large air bubbles but do not worry about little undulations which will flatten out as the paper dries.

Wet the gumstrip with a moist sponge, brush or garden spray. Make sure you don't wipe off the gum, it should feel sticky to your fingers. No glue left on the tape is another cause of failure!

Overlap the paper with approximately half the gumstrip. Press down firmly, being careful not to rub and damage the wet paper. See fig. 62.

Leave to dry horizontal. Leaving to dry upright or attempting to stretch paper on walls is a recipe for failure as the paper will split. The water drains by gravity; the top part of the paper dries faster than the rest and will split from the resultant tension. If you have to attempt it, try to dry the paper evenly with a hair dryer.

The paper will dry naturally between 4 and 12 hours.

Stretch paper on both sides of the board. Preparation is always quicker in multiples!

Having stretched one side, turn the board over and stand it on four film canisters/ink bottles or something similar at the four corners (not on the paper), so the board has air circulating round it. Both sides can then dry normally. Stretch the second sheet as before.

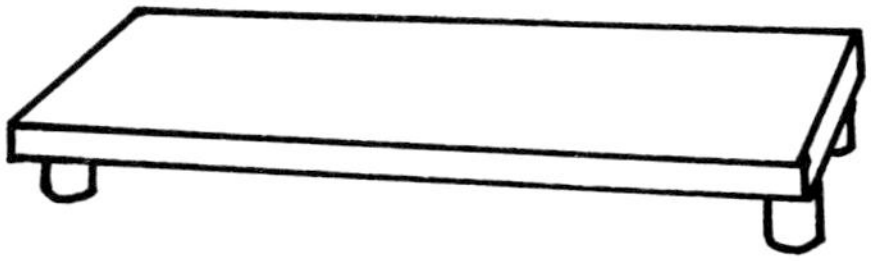

65. *Board standing on canisters.*

ii. On an open frame

Paper can be stretched on an open frame up to approximately 150 × 150 cm (5 × 5′) before the tension becomes too great and the paper splits.

The frame

Make a well jointed and glued chassis using approximately 57 × 16 mm ($2\frac{1}{4} \times \frac{5}{8}$″) wood for small sizes, increasing dimensions of wood with size of chassis. Use a waterproof glue for joints. See *List of sources* (page 165), if you cannot make your own chassis.

An oily wood like teak will not need sizing but any other will need a coat of shellac on the side used when it is new, to prevent the glue sinking in (see page 76).

It is a little awkward though not impossible to use both sides of the chassis at the same time with this method. I find it easier to use one side at a time.

Stretching the paper

Glue is used instead of gumstrip, unless you have a wide enough frame for the gumstrip to fit on.

Scotch glue (also Pearl glue) is used because it can be washed off the frame with water afterwards. Any water-soluble glue can be used, e.g. vegetarians may prefer to use starch.

66. *Scotch glue granules.*

Scotch glue is a very cheap animal glue. Soak 5 g in 56 ml (2 fl oz) of water for approximately three hours, until the granules have absorbed as much water as they can. They will be the same pale colour all the way through. Melt the mixture in a double boiler without boiling. See page 18 for a full explanation of using and heating animal glue. This is enough glue for a frame 100 × 100 cm (39 × 39″).

Cut the paper to the outside dimensions of the chassis. Soak and drain it as in *method i.*, fig. 64.

Meanwhile paint the sized side of the chassis with the melted glue.

Place the drained paper over the glued chassis and press down well (without rubbing) all the way round. Try to get it as flat as possible particularly on larger chassis. For large chassis this can be easier if you clamp it in a forward tilting easel, attach the top edge first and as the paper hangs flat press down the sides and bottom edge. Remove the chassis from the easel and leave to dry flat. See page 78 for reasons why.

67. *Stretched paper:* Left: *on open frame (painting area within pencilled keyline);* Right: *on board (painting area within gumstrip). Also showing a heavy metal straight edge.*

Reusing boards and chassis

Cutting off the work

Use a sharp Stanley knife and a heavy metal straight edge. Lay the straight edge on the work side of the gumstrip or glued edge, so that any slips don't slice into the work.

On large works, particularly on open frames, cut two opposite sides first, followed by the next two. This reduces the risk of the paper splitting diagonally as the tension is released.

If the picture is to be framed, cut off part of the gumstrip margin so you won't lose any of the painting under the edge of the frame.

Cleaning the board/chassis

Cover the gumstrip or glued paper edge in water for approximately 20 minutes, using a sponge or a garden spray. (Could be longer for heavy paper). It will then lift off in seconds with a paint scraper. Don't bother picking at the half-soaked gumstrip/paper edge because it lifts off so easily when fully soaked.

Rinse over the board or chassis with a clean sponge and you're ready to start again.

68. *Paint scraper lifting off wet gumstrip.*

Failure

If you have a failure, you can reuse the paper.

From a board, cut off the paper including the gumstrip. The gumstrip will come off when you soak the paper, leaving you with the original size sheet.

Only the paper on the inside of a chassis can be saved.

Using a wet ground

If you want to paint into wet paper, then take the precaution of leaving the stretched paper to dry thoroughly beforehand in case it fails. Once you know it's successful you can wet it again with a sponge or garden spray.

WATERCOLOUR AND GOUACHE PAINT

The binder for watercolour

The binder for watercolours is basically gum kordofan with the addition of plasticizers, wetting agents and preservatives. See gum kordofan and glycerine (fig. 54).

Gum kordofan is a type of gum acacia, obtained from acacia trees which grow in Kordofan, a district of Africa. Gum kordofan is more flexible and transparent and less soluble than other acacias which makes it more suitable for watercolour and gum tempera.

Gum arabic is a type of gum acacia. It is a loose name for any gum acacia.

The binder should be transparent because the paint film is so thin. The little amount of pigment which is deposited needs no hindrances. Dextrin is used as a cheaper substitute for kordofan but it is white, so it can extend the pigmentation. See *Appendix A* for brand details (page 149).

The binder for gouache

The binder for gouache is basically the same as for watercolour. Part of the gum is usually replaced by some dextrin (made from starch). This can be for economy. But dextrin also imparts smoothness, brushing quality and opacity which are desirable gouache qualities. An excess of dextrin can also be detrimental to the stability of the paint film. Any extending tendency of the pigmentation can be ignored because of the addition of white pigment. See *Gouache* in *Pigments and the paint*, page 82.

Pigments and the paint

Permanent pigments should be used.

Pigments which are sensitive to atmospheric pollution should be avoided because of the lack of protection from the binder in watercolour and gouache and the fact that the pictures are not varnished. See *Pigment list*, page 131.

See *Discussion of artists' materials, particularly paints* (page 7) and *Appendix A* (page 150).

Watercolour

All pigments have slightly reduced lightfastness in watercolour because the paint film is so thin. However, if pigments with Blue Wool Scale numbers of 7 or 8 are used this should not be a problem. See pigments chapter (page 128) for further explanation.

Remember that opaque pigments appear more transparent because they are applied in thin films.

Gouache

Because gouache (often called 'designer's colours') is popular with designers and graphic artists whose work is generally of a temporary nature, some fugitive colours are used for their short-lived brilliance. These are marked by the manufacturers as poor in lightfastness. See *Appendix A* (page 150) for specific indication of lightfastness in gouache ranges.

Gouache is rendered opaque by the mixing of white pigment into each dry colour. This is not extending the pigment. It is supposed to be an opaque medium. Some manufacturers claim they achieve the opacity of some colours by loading the binder with the maximum amount of pure pigment, i.e. without white.

Pigments which have reduced lightfastness when used half-strength (quarter-strength etc) should not be used in gouache because of the amount of white pigment used to produce opacity, i.e. those with Blue Wool Scale numbers of 7 or 8 should be used instead.

Making your own watercolours and gouache

This is possible for economic or aesthetic reasons or for unusual colours mixed from dry pigments. Patience is required to obtain the right strength binder for each pigment (or the paint will go hard and become insoluble) and to grind the colours finely so that coloured washes result and not gritty ones.

See *Bibliography* (page 172) for sources of recipes.

The paint

Watercolour

Watercolour paint comes in pans and tubes. Millilitre for millilitre, tube colours are cheaper than pan colours but it is easier to waste tube colours.

69. *Watercolour paint:* Left to right: *Half pan, whole pan; and tube.*

Amount of plasticizer

The amount of plasticizer in pans or tubes varies from brand to brand. The plasticizer is usually glycerine but can also be honey. The plasticizer improves flexibility, brushability and solubility but it is hygroscopic. It should not be used in excess or the paper is apt to go mouldy, especially in humid countries.

You may find you like to choose pans or tubes according to their relative solubility. More plasticizer means the colours dissolve more easily from the pans but are used up quicker, and dry paint can be dissolved subsequently more easily.

More plasticizer also makes the paint slower drying, duller and more transparent.

See *Appendix A* (page 149) for relative plasticizer levels.

Gouache

Gouache comes in tubes only. The amount of plasticizer is kept to a mininum because of its tendency to dull the colour and make it more transparent.

Thinners

The thinners for watercolour and gouache is distilled water which should be used when painting. Metals and salts in tap water can effect the gum and cause the pigments to separate from the binder, leaving dusty, unbound pigment on the paper surface. Distilled water is not just boiled water, it is produced by collecting the steam from boiling water. See *List of sources* (page 166).

Mediums

Watercolour

Gum arabic solutions (probably kordofan) are available as a type of medium for watercolour. These should be used extremely sparingly. The manufacturer has balanced the amount of binder in each colour to make each paint as stable as possible. The more you interfere the less stable the paint becomes. A lot of gum makes the paint layer quite brittle and resoluble to subsequent layers. This could be used to advantage if you want to dissolve parts of the painting away, i.e. use it as a type of resist. It would not remain in the actual painting then. This method can be a little more subtle than using masking fluid.

Gouache

There are no mediums for gouache, though there is nothing against using gum solution in the same way as suggested for watercolour.

Making gum solution

Gum solution can be made by crushing with a hammer, 28 g (1 oz) of gum kordofan wrapped in a cloth. Combine gum with 56 ml (2 fl oz) of hot distilled water in a jar and leave it to dissolve, between 3–12 hours. Strain the solution through a tea strainer to remove unwanted bits of bark.

Using gouache

Gouache should not be used for a real impasto effect, an appreciable thickness of gouache is likely to crack. Its characteristic opacity and mattness provides an illusion of body.

CARE OF A WATERCOLOUR OR GOUACHE PAINTING

Varnishing

Watercolours and gouaches should not be varnished because of the difficulty in removing the varnish when necessary.

Framing

Watercolours and gouaches should be either stored away or hung in glazed frames. See *Appendix C* (page 160) for information on the necessary type of storage or frame.

Rolling watercolour and gouache paintings

Watercolour and gouache paintings should not be rolled because the gum binder is not flexible enough. Paintings should be transported flat.

Chapter 6
GESSO GROUNDS

Genuine gesso offers an alternative ground for oil painting and is the ground used for tempera painting. It can also be used for any of the other media. Gesso boards can be bought but are expensive. You can make them cheaply and one of the advantages of gesso is that it is so adjustable to personal needs. See *List of sources*, page 165.

SUPPORT

Gesso needs a rigid support as it is not flexible enough for use on canvas. Canvas mounted on board is a possibility but the glowing surface of tempera would be reduced by the canvas weave.

Originally, hardwoods were used to make panels but these have been superseded by machine-made boards because of greater stability and savings in timber costs and preparation time. See *Bibliography* (page 172) for sources on preparation of hardwood panels.

A board provides a rigid, keyed surface for the gesso to grip.

Types of board

MDF (Medium density fibreboard) is made from pressed wood fibre. It cannot split down the grain as it has none. The corners of the thicker boards, 9 mm ($\frac{3}{8}''$) or more, will not dent easily. It comes in thicknesses from 2–30 mm ($\frac{1}{16}$–$1\frac{1}{4}''$) and has two smooth sides. MDF is cheaper than plywood and slightly more than blockboard. It takes screws well.

Hardboard is also pressed wood fibre. Details are the same as for MDF but it only comes in thicknesses from 2–6 mm ($\frac{1}{16}$–$\frac{1}{4}''$) and has one smooth side only. The corners are susceptible to denting if the board is dropped. There are two types of hardboard, tempered and untempered. Tempered has been prepared with oil. Provided it is prepared as advised, tempered hardboard appears to be more durable in the long run. It is only slightly more expensive than untempered. Hardboard is the cheapest board, partly because it is so thin. It is best used for gesso boards which are less than 60 cm (2 ft) square. See page 87.

Sundeala *A* This is also pressed wood fibre. Details are the same as for MDF but it only comes in thicknesses from 6–12 mm ($\frac{1}{4}$–$\frac{1}{2}''$) and has one smooth side only. Sundeala *A* quality is recommended for artists because Sundeala *K* is too absorbent. Corners are less likely to be dented than hardboard, but Sundeala is softer than the other boards of the same thickness. It is more expensive than MDF but is lighter in weight.

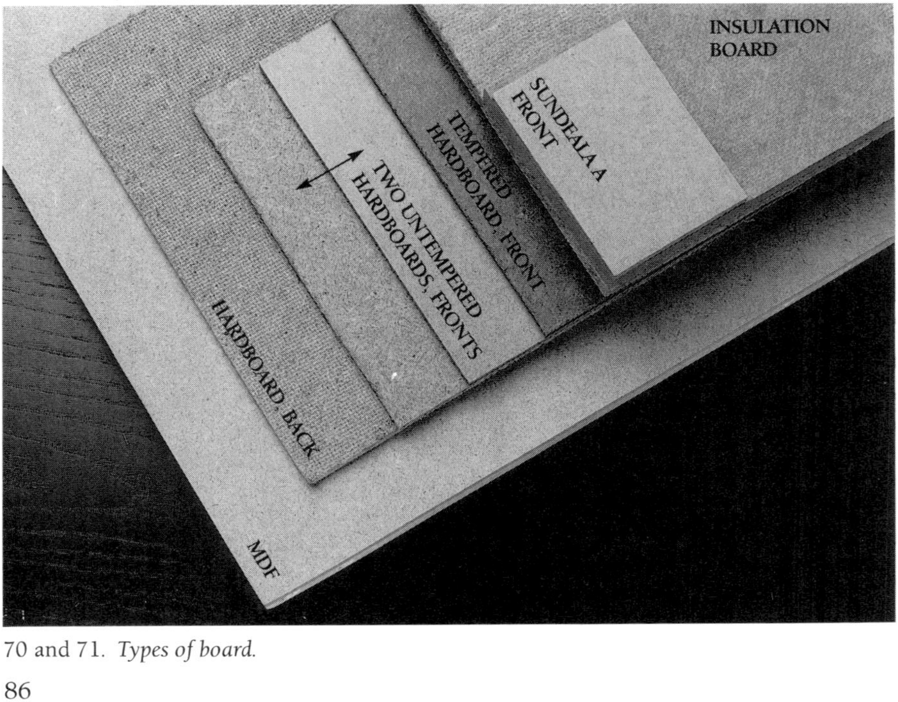

70 and 71. *Types of board.*

Insulation board (Softboard) is a weak wood fibre board which is not recommended for artists.

Plywood is made of various numbers of thin layers of wood and/or veneers (plys), the grain of each laying at right angles to one another. Over a period of time, the outer veneer sometimes splits in fine lines down the grain which show as cracks in the painting, particularly through oil grounds and gesso. The corners of the thicker boards, 9 mm ($\frac{3}{8}$″) or more, will not dent easily. It can be susceptible to slight warping. It comes in a large number of thicknesses depending on the number of plys and has two smooth sides. WBP (weather and boil proof) or marine quality are those recommended if you do use plywood.

Blockboard is made of small lengths of wood sandwiched between two outer skins of wood veneer or plywood. The top veneer can split like plywood. The corners will not dent easily and blockboard is unlikely to warp. It comes in thicknesses from 13–26 mm ($\frac{1}{2}$–1″) and has two smooth sides. The quality of blockboard varies a lot. A poor quality board will show gaps in its edge where the inside structure should be. Well structured five-ply is recommended if you do use blockboard.

Chipboard is made of pressed wood chips. It does not have any grain. It is liable to break or chip rather than dent, particularly around the edges. It comes in thicknesses from 6–38 mm ($\frac{1}{4}$–1$\frac{1}{2}$″) and various densities from 600–720 (kg per cubic metre) and up. Heavier densities are recommended if you are going to use it. It has the poorest surface stability out of all the boards, particles can come away from the front and the colour of the wood chips can seep through into the ground, but it is the cheapest thick board. It does not take screws well.

Sterling board has similar disadvantages to chipboard.

All the boards are likely to bend from their own weight in large sheets, i.e. 244 × 122 cm (8 × 4′).

Initial construction and preparation of support

Boards

Man-made boards will warp, particularly when being prepared with water-based size or primer.

If the board is smaller than 60 × 60 cm (2 × 2′) then both sides are prepared the same. This equal tension on both sides will keep the board flat. Use 3 mm ($\frac{1}{8}$″) hardboard for these smaller boards because it is the cheapest.

Larger sizes will need to be braced by attaching them to independent frames. This is a type of cradled board. Make a well-jointed and glued frame using approximately 57 × 16 mm (2$\frac{1}{4}$ × $\frac{5}{8}$″) wood for small sizes, increasing dimensions of wood with size of chassis. Use square-edged wood so the board has the maximum amount of frame to join to (fig. 73). Use a crossbar for sizes bigger than approximately 71 × 91 cm (28 × 36″) and multiple crossbars as the size of chassis increases. See *List of sources* (page 165) if you cannot make your own frames.

Thin boards, e.g. 3 mm ($\frac{1}{8}$″) hardboard, should not be attached from the front using

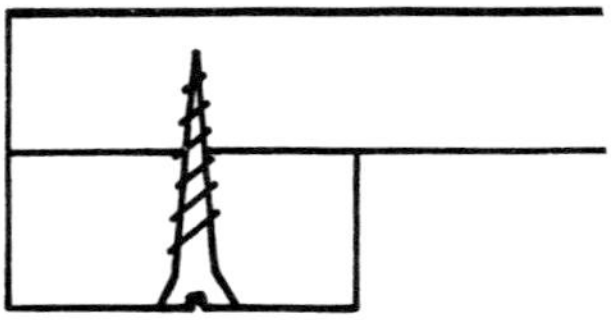

73. *Cross-section of chassis and board showing screw and square-edged wood for maximum attachment.*

72. *Chassis with crossbars.*

74. *Cradled boards, front and back.*

panel pins. The ground never takes over the pins, even when they have been punched below the surface and filled. Using cocktail sticks instead of panel pins may be better, but a thick board eliminates the problem. Use a board which is at least 9 mm ($\frac{3}{8}''$) thick in order for the screw to get enough grip from the back.

Cut the board to fit the outside dimensions of the chassis.

Use a proprietary wood glue to glue and screw the chassis and board together.

Any fuzzy edges on the board from the saw can be neatened with a coarse file.

Either side of any board can be used.

Degreasing boards

Once constructed, the side to be gessoed and edges of the board should be scrubbed with a clean rag and methylated spirits to degrease them. Wear rubber gloves because methylated spirits is toxic by skin absorption. If it's an uncradled board, do both sides and the edges. Doing the back as well means you can't transfer the grease from there to the front. A greasy board can resist the gesso and cause pin-holes. Leave to dry thoroughly for an hour or two.

Tempered hardboard must be degreased very thoroughly, so no greasy patches are left.

Sanding boards

Boards should be sanded using a medium-fine (4/0–6/0 grain) garnet paper to provide a key for the gesso to grip. Garnet paper cuts better than glass paper. Be careful to sand the surface evenly or the board will absorb size or gesso unevenly.

Canvas on board

See oil painting chapter for types of canvas and mounting canvas on board (pages 11, 22).

A cradled board is best because it will withstand better the tension from the cloth on the front. If using an uncradled board, do apply a coat of gesso to the reverse, otherwise the board will warp.

Using plywood and blockboard

To prevent the hair-line cracks in the wood-grain from showing through, a layer of muslin can be glued on to the board with the size. The gesso will cover the muslin. This does not always work and the cracks can still manage to transfer themselves through to the gesso and the painting.

Note on using canvas or muslin on board

Any cloth on the board is an extra element in the ground which can go wrong. Canvas on board should only be used if you need the weave of the canvas with gesso.

Avoiding plywood and blockboard would seem more sensible than trying to offset the transference of hair-line cracks by using muslin.

Muslin is sometimes recommended to give the gesso something extra to grip. A properly made gesso can grip a degreased and sanded board quite well enough without this extra element. Try chipping some gesso off your board; you will see its grip is quite sufficient. It may even pull away with it some of the wood fibre.

GROUNDS

Gesso is made of animal glue and an inert pigment or a mixture of white pigment and inert pigments. See alternative binders and pigments (pages 97, 98).

Glue

N.B. Read *Sizing canvas* (page 18) for extra explanation on using and understanding rabbit-skin glue.

Similar to when rabbit-skin glue is prepared for sizing canvas, the measurements of glue and water can only be approximate, the glue must be made in a double boiler, and its set must be tested.

The measurements will probably be between 70–85 g ($2\frac{1}{2}$–3 oz) of glue to 1.137 litres (2 pints) of water. This will be enough gesso to cover approximately a 122 × 152 cm (4 × 5′) board. If the glue is made too weak the gesso will be too soft and powder off the board. If it is made too strong the gesso will be too hard and brittle and will chip/crack off the board.

Make up several boards at a time. Depending on the size of the board, of course, 4 or 5 boards will take about the same time as one!

Making the glue

As a starting point put 80 g (3 oz) of glue with 1.137 litres (2 pints) of water in the top part of a clean double boiler. Leave to swell for approximately 2 hours until it is a uniform beige colour. Keep the lid on the double boiler!

Melt the glue and leave to set in a cool place. Test it when it is at room temperature, otherwise it might appear stronger than it really is.

The set glue should look and feel like fruit jelly except a split in it with your finger should be firm and rough rather than smooth and tough.

If the jelly is too strong it needs more water. If the jelly resembles size, then it is too weak and needs some more glue. Add more glue or water if necessary and repeat the process until the right set is obtained. Note the proportions so you can make the glue in one go next time.

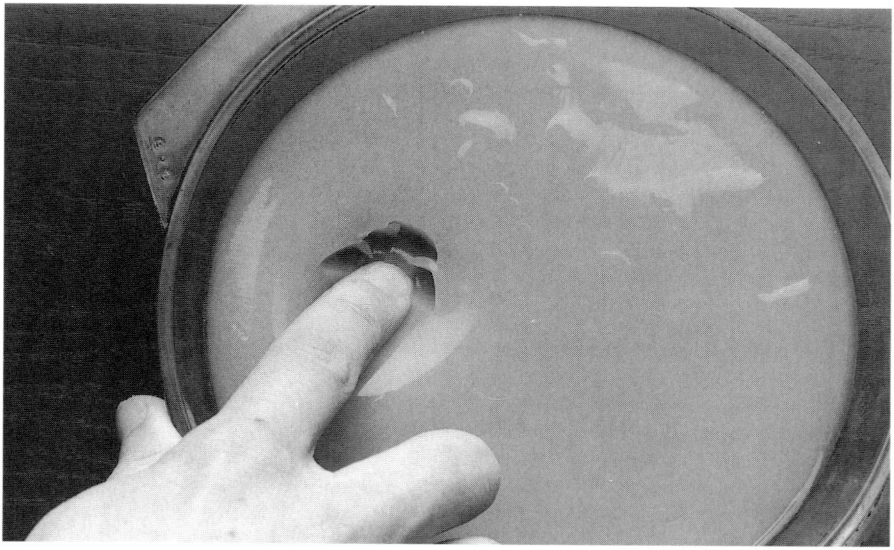

75. *Split glue for gesso.*

Sizing the board

The board needs sizing in order to reduce its absorbency. Tempered hardboard does not need sizing because it is not absorbent. Without size the glue in the gesso would sink into the board and leave a weak layer of pigment on top. The edges of man-made boards are often more susceptible to moisture than the faces. An initial sizing helps to equalize this difference and make for a more stable board. Sizing may also help to isolate any greasiness still on the board and prevent pin-holes.

If using part of the glue made for the gesso it will need to be diluted with 50% hot water to make it size strength (see page 19). Some sources claim boards need a stronger size solution. If you find your gesso sinking into the board then increase the strength of the size used.

Heat the glue in the double boiler until it feels hot to your finger; do not boil. **Hot** glue will size the board most efficiently by penetrating it more.

Use a 7 cm ($2\frac{3}{4}''$) varnishing brush and put the size on sparingly. A flood will have the same defects as too strong a size. Size one side and the edges first and leave the board to dry flat. Once dry enough to turn over, size the other size and leave to dry thoroughly, between 3–12 hours. If the board is cradled then the back does not need to be sized.

Making the gesso

Gesso needs to be white in order for the painting on it to be as bright as possible and remain so. Gesso does not need to be mulled because the pigments chosen disperse well in the glue on their own.

White pigment alone does not disperse well in the glue and is relatively expensive. Whiting forms a good dispersion, dries to a fairly white finish and is relatively cheap.

76. *Gesso at thin single cream consistency.*

See page 98 for functions of different pigments.

Replacing 10% of the whiting with titanium white will improve the whiteness and opacity of the gesso without affecting its structure. Start with approximately 450 g (1 lb) of whiting and 50 g (2 oz) of titanium. Mix these together whilst dry to disperse the titanium. This will make enough gesso for 3–4 coats on a 152 × 122 cm (5 × 4′) board.

Heat the glue until hot. Transfer the glue into a spare pan and put the pigment mixture in the top half of the double boiler. Keep the double boiler on the lowest heat setting. With no heat at all or a lack of it the gesso will harden; but you mustn't let it boil either! Pour enough glue into the mixed pigment to stir it into a lump free paste. Make sure the pigment is thoroughly wet and mixed. Dilute with the glue until the gesso is the consistency of a very thin single cream. Keep the lid on from now on or the gesso will thicken up and skin over from water evaporation.

Using the gesso

Gesso is used by building up layers, usually about five and not less than three, to obtain a structure of decent thickness. Several thin layers are more stable than one thick one. Make the gesso in the morning so you can complete the boards in one day. The gesso is bound to skin if you keep it overnight and there is better adhesion between layers if they are done in succession. Pin-holes can develop if new gesso is added over a dry coat.

If the gesso thickens during the day because of evaporation of water (from the glue) then add a little hot/warm water (not glue) to keep it at a very thin single cream consistency. Otherwise the glue, and hence the gesso will become too strong. It is important to keep the gesso the same strength (or if anything weaker) because stronger layers applied over weaker ones may cause them to crack and pull the gesso off the board. This is the 'gradation of layers' rule.

Stir the gesso before applying another layer to prevent the pigment settling at the bottom of the pan. Try not to whip air bubbles in, as pin-holes can result (see page 99).

A 7 cm ($2\frac{3}{4}$″) varnishing brush gives a good even layer with minimum brushmarks. Do not brush the first coat on vigorously or the size will lift up. Brush on the first coat, including the edges, then go over it with your fingers rubbing it into the board. This makes a good bond and helps to prevent pin-holes. See fig. 77.

Rinse the brush out between each coat or it will set hard before the next one. The gesso will dry to the touch in 10–20 minutes.

If the board is uncradled turn it over and repeat on the reverse. Do apply an even number of coats on both sides, missing out just one from one side can make the board warp. Only do the edges when you do a coat on the front or they'll be double thickness!

Just build the layers up one by one, including the edges, on a cradled board. For the second coat just brush on and leave to touch dry. Drying time can get a bit longer as the layers build up. Brush the third and subsequent coats on at right angles to the previous coat. This helps to produce a level gesso ground.

Keep going until the gesso is 1–2 mm ($\frac{1}{16}$″) thick or more, so that the dry gesso is thick enough to sand. Leave to dry thoroughly, between 12–24 hours.

77. *First coat of gesso on board.*

78. *Gesso board.*

Stippled or patterned gesso

For a randomly modelled gesso the last couple of coats can be applied by stippling them on vertically with a wavy mottler. See fig. 25.

For patterned gesso the last coat can be surfaced by pressing a piece of cloth/canvas or a sheet of glasspaper into the soft but not wet gesso.

Incised, carved and sanded gesso

A wet gesso board can be incised with any number of tools in order to model it.

A dry gesso board can be carved/engraved. Sanding can also be a way of modelling it.

A good thickness of gesso on the board will prevent you from going through to the board. If the gesso needs sizing for the medium you are using, either do this after you have modelled the surface or if you re-model the gesso when painting then carefully re-size any areas you need to. See page 94 for sizing gesso, and acrylic chapter, page 46.

Applying gesso to canvas on board

Apply the gesso as thinly as possible. A wavy mottler is good. Thick layers are more brittle and will fill in the weave of the canvas and cover it up! This would counteract the point of gluing the canvas on in the first place.

Surfaced (or toothed) gesso for pastels, charcoal and other drawing materials

This can be done by adding one of the inert pigments which imparts tooth to the last one or two coats of gesso. See list (page 98). Keep this addition to no more than 10% to keep the structural advantages of the whiting gesso.

Mix the extra pigment with some glue before adding it to the main batch as the new pigment will not disperse well on its own and will make lumps in the gesso.

Don't sand the board as you'll remove the surface!

Any size required is applied over the toothed surface.

Alternative method for a smoother surfaced gesso

Soak a pumice stone in warm water for approximately 15 minutes. Use the wet stone to rub over the gesso board. The gesso board will partly dissolve and some pumice will be deposited in it. Leave to dry.

Finishing the board

For tempera painting (also for encaustic and silverpoint)

Acrylics, watercolour, gouache and inks can be used on unsized gesso depending on the effect desired.

Tempera painting needs a flat ivory-like finish if the paint is to optimize its glowing skin-like quality. There is no structural objection to an unsanded or textured board if you want that effect.

Once dry, the front of the gesso board can be sanded to remove brushmarks. Use a medium-fine (4/0–6/0 grain) garnet paper wrapped round a block if you want a dead flat surface. Garnet paper cuts better than glass paper. Dispense with the block if you want slight undulations. Keep going until all the brushmarks have gone. Do the edges too if you want them neatened up.

To produce the ivory-like effect get a clean damp lint-free rag (the cloth must not deposit any fluff into the gesso) and wrap it into a smooth pad. A piece of worn cotton sheeting is good. Rub over the board in a light circular motion. This polishes the gesso by dissolving the top layer and spreading it out to fill in any scratches. Keep going until a sheen is built up.

Sizing gesso

For tempera: With experience you may want or need to reduce the absorbency of the gesso. Use a gelatin size (see below). Keep notes on strength of size so you can repeat or change the effect.

Note: Sizing boards in this way will also be necessary for use with watercolour, gouache or inks if you want to achieve handling properties similar to using these media on paper. Sizing can be done after a preliminary drawing of silverpoint, charcoal or graphite. See page 46 for sizing gesso for acrylics.

For oil painting: The board may be left as it is after its final coat of gesso or can be sanded and/or polished as for tempera. At this point the gesso is too absorbent for oil paint. The oil in the paint would continue to sink into the gesso whilst the paint was drying, leaving the pigment insufficiently bound on the surface. The gesso needs to be sized to achieve just the right slight absorbency for oil paint.

Gesso on canvas on board also needs sizing.

A weak gelatin size is used. Gelatin does not interfere structurally. It is transparent so the whiteness of the gesso will not be impaired.

Technical gelatin is easier to use than food gelatin which is weaker. Technical gelatin may sometimes be in capsules rather than sheet form.

If too strong a size is used the oil paint will slip over the surface and not grip the ground. If the size is too weak the oil paint will sink into the gesso. Either will affect the handling properties of the paint.

Gelatin size: Measure 15 g ($\frac{1}{2}$ oz) gelatin and soak it in 600 ml (1 pint) of water in the top of a double boiler for approximately 2 hours. This will be enough size for the number of boards made from 1.137 litres (2 pints) of gesso, i.e. the measurements in this chapter.

Melt it in a double boiler and leave to cool.

Although the size is most evenly distributed whilst it is hot, it cannot be used hot as it would dissolve the top layer of gesso. Therefore it is left until cool but not set and then brushed on using a 7 cm ($2\frac{3}{4}$") varnishing brush. Do the edges as well to give the same surface to paint on right up to and over the edge if required.

Leave to dry, usually between 2–6 hours.

The gelatin size will not last more than a week in the fridge before it starts to decompose. Throw away what you don't use and make fresh next time.

If the paint seems to be sinking when using the board with oil paint, see *Sinking oil paint . . .* (page 35). For the next panel either put two coats of size on, letting the first dry, or increase the strength of the size by 5 g of gelatin.

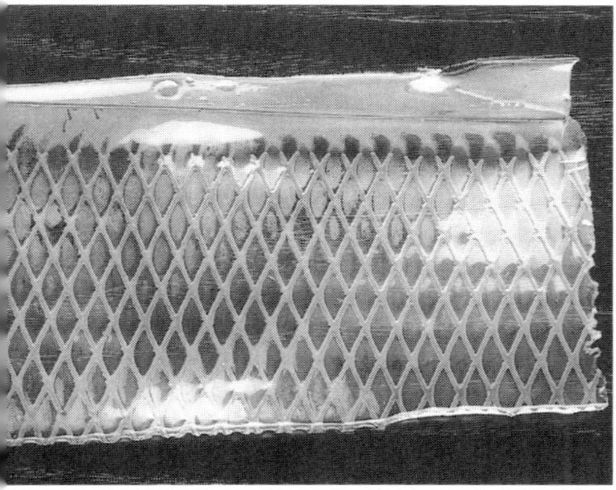

79. *Technical gelatin.*

80. *Cool, but not set gelatin.*

Using shellac for sizing

Shellac is not recommended because it darkens and embrittles.

Final precaution for bracing uncradled boards

For the ultimate in bracing uncradled boards you can size the final coat on the back with gelatin and then put on a layer of paint, i.e. the medium used for the painting on the front. Any movement will then affect both sides in the same way.

Coloured grounds

There is no structural objection to coloured grounds, the effects are optical.

Any transparent media need to be used on a white ground so that the maximum amount of light is reflected back and the painting will appear and remain as bright as possible. In fact an oil painting will get brighter on a white ground. A pale beige opaque, coloured ground is the most suitable colour if you do not want the painting to become brighter.

Opaque media do not need to be used on a white ground because the light doesn't travel beyond the pigment layer. The brightness of the media comes from the reflection of light from the pigments themselves.

Method i. should be used for any transparent media, whilst either method could be used for opaque media.

Method i. In order to colour gesso for a transparent technique, a veil is applied using a transparent pigment in a second coat of gelatin size. If you colour the first coat of size the colour will sink too deeply into the gesso. This will negate the white ground.

Having chosen the colour you want, mull the pigments with water until you have a smooth paste. See tempera chapter for photographs and extra explanation (figs. 46–49). Any additional water used in mulling the pigment will weaken the size. The first coat has already sized the board sufficiently and it is safer to have a weaker layer than a stronger one. See *Gradation of layers* (page 92).

Mix the pigment paste into the cool but not set size and brush on a second coat quickly. Then wipe the board over with a cloth to even up the colour. Leave to dry, between 6–12 hours.

In the photograph (fig. 81) a more pigmented size was used on the darker board, which was only lightly sanded and the coloured size layer was wiped well with the cloth. A less pigmented size was used on the lighter board which was on a thoroughly sanded board.

Method ii. An opaque, coloured ground can be made by mixing any pigment of your choice (transparent or opaque) into the gesso for the last one or two coats. Mix the extra pigment with some glue before adding it to the main batch as the new pigment will not disperse well on its own. Try to use only about 10% coloured pigment so as not to interfere with the sound structure of the whiting gesso. If the board is to be sanded then apply 3 or 4 coats to ensure you don't sand back to the white, or use coloured gesso from the start.

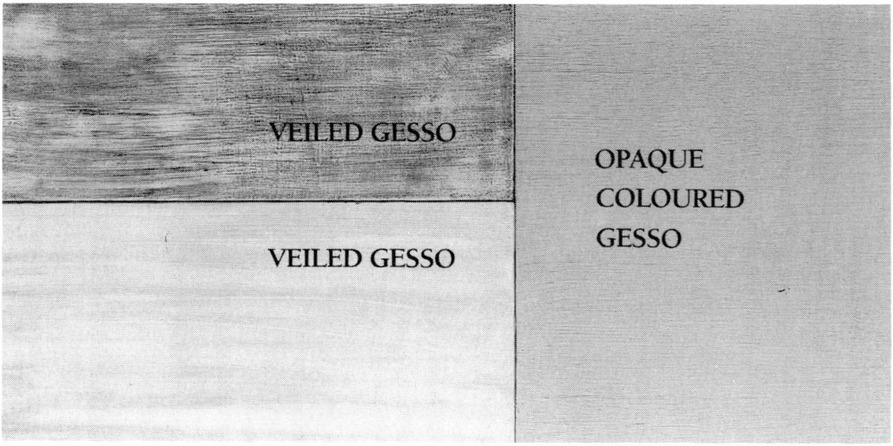

81. *Coloured gesso grounds.*

Coloured and toothed gesso

Gesso can be coloured and toothed by a combination of both methods.

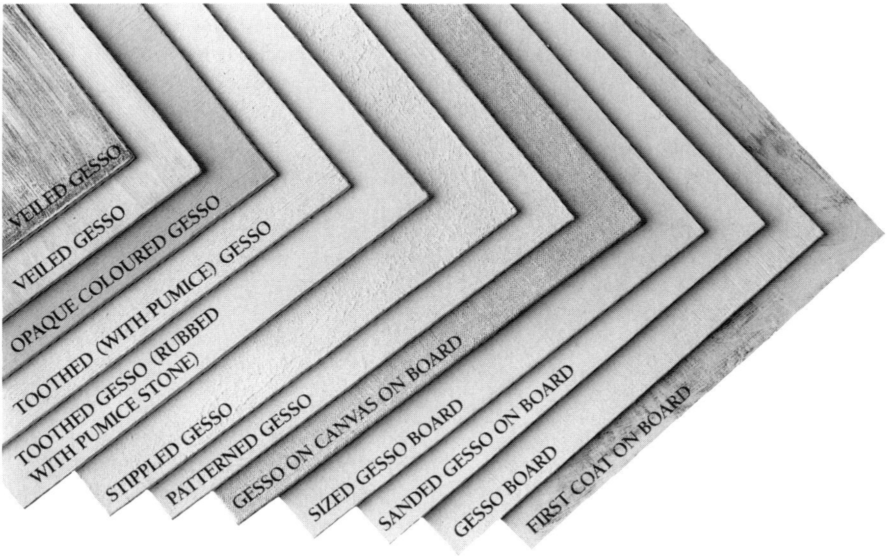

82. *Types of gesso board.*

OTHER BINDERS FOR GESSO

Calf-skin glue, is a rabbit-skin glue type but it is not readily available.
Blended glues (a mixture of more than one type) are also rabbit-skin glue types.
Gelatin produces a weaker gesso than rabbit-skin glue.
Parchment clippings can be used to make a glue.
Casein produces a more brittle gesso but is made and applied without heat, which may be an advantage. See *Bibliography* for sources on preparation (page 171).

83. *Parchment clippings and casein.*

Glycerine or honey should not be used in gesso in an effort to increase flexibility. Their hygroscopicity can damage the gesso structurally.

Synthetic resins have definite scope for use in gesso but we await any research on the subject.

Manufactured gesso powders tend to produce a rather splintery gesso and do not offer the control that studio-made gesso does. See *List of sources*, page 166.

OTHER PIGMENTS USED IN GESSO

Other inert pigments can be used in gesso to impart extra tooth, texture, smoothness or absorbency. Unless the list below states that whiting can be replaced, it is suggested you use approximately 10% of the said pigment because they do not disperse as well as whiting (or the pigments which can replace whiting). Only replace more than 10% of the whiting if you need to and certainly don't go beyond 40%.

You could use one or more of the pigments from below throughout the whole gesso batch, or you could use them in the gesso for the last couple of coats. If doing the latter, mix the pigment/s with some glue before adding it to the main gesso as the new pigment will not disperse well on its own.

The pigments are listed alphabetically in the pigment list (page 131). Their uses in gesso are:

Barium sulphate: Gives tooth.
Blanc fixe: Gives tooth.
China clay: Very smooth gesso.
Flake White: is extremely toxic in its dry form. It is neither as white nor so opaque as titanium.
Gypsum: Produces an all round poorer gesso than whiting.
Magnesium calcium carbonate: Can be used but not recommended.
Marble: Gives tooth and a white gesso.
Mica: Does not produce a stable gesso.
Plaster of Paris: Used slaked and replacing whiting, this produces a very smooth, fine-grained gesso called gesso sottile. See *Bibliography* for sources on preparation (page 171).
Precipitated chalk: Finer grain gesso than whiting, which it can replace. It is more expensive. It is not recommended for gelatin gesso, the combination of fine particles and weak size prevents the gesso forming.
Pumice: Gives tooth and off-white gesso.
Red bole: Very smooth, opaque red gesso.
Silica: Gives tooth to gesso.
Talc: Does not produce a structurally sound gesso.
Whiting: On its own will be less white than with some titanium or zinc added. Recommended for gelatin gesso as its coarser particles help form the gesso.
Zinc white: Can be used instead of titanium but is neither so white nor so opaque.

PROBLEMS WITH GESSO GROUNDS

The method given in this chapter is an amalgamation of information which should result in trouble-free gesso boards. Reasons for this method are given throughout the chapter but the following extra notes may help in case of any problems.

General problems

Damp or excessively cold rooms can cause all sorts of problems and so can the wrong strength of glue. The 'right' strength is dealt with on page 89.

Pin-holes

These tiny pinpricks in the surface of the gesso can prevent you getting a smooth ground for tempera paint. They cannot always be removed by sanding.

84. *Pin-holes in gesso.*

Pin-holes can be caused by any of the following:

Air bubbles within the gesso can cause pin-holes when the gesso is brushed on. This can be from tipping the pigment into the glue and stirring too much air in. Bubbling gesso from too much heat will also trap air bubbles but the gesso should never be that near boiling point!

Pin-holes can also be caused by applying new gesso to thoroughly dry gesso. Try to complete the gessoing in one day.

Some sources claim pin-holes may also be caused by too great a surface tension in the gesso. Even if this is true there is no satisfactory way of breaking surface tension. Alcohol should not be added as it can have a detrimental effect on the gesso structure. Ox-gall should not be used because it would sensitize the gesso. i.e. make it dissolve too easily.

Also, see *Index* under *Pin-holes in gesso.*

Gesso is too gritty

Gesso can be gritty or granular if the pigment is too coarse or is not suspended evenly in the glue. Sanding the gesso board may just leave a minutely pitted surface which will interfere visually with tempera.

This can be avoided by mulling the pigment with water (see page 63) until you have a smooth paste before mixing it into the gesso. Try to offset this use of water by using a proportionately smaller amount of water to make the glue with. This is obviously fiddly because of not necessarily using all the glue mixture for your mulled pigment. Do the best you can.

Alternatively, if you leave the mixture on the plate (for a few days) to evaporate off, you will have a finer ground pigment which will not be gritty and should disperse better.

Top layers of gesso cracking

This is due to the glue being stronger in the top coats compared to the previous ones. See *Using the gesso* (page 92) for full explanation.

Gesso cracking throughout

This can happen if one of the layers of gesso was too thick or if the room was too cold and damp.

Cracks occurring once the gesso is over a year old are probably caused by the support moving.

HALF-CHALK OR EMULSION GROUNDS

In an effort to adapt gesso for canvas on open stretchers and principally oil paint, a half-chalk ground has developed.

This consists of mixing oil into gesso. This does increase its flexibility but does not make it as flexible as an oil ground. It also reduces the absorbency of the ground. The whiteness of the ground is initially less than gesso. Any flexibility decreases rapidly. A half-chalk ground becomes almost as brittle as a gesso ground after a few years. The ground is much more hygroscopic than an oil ground on an open stretcher. This also encourages the ground to crack.

The absorbency is apt to vary from batch to batch even when using the same recipe and problems with sinking are frequent. In other words there is a very narrow margin for error, e.g. different batches of chalk produce different absorbencies in the ground.

The half-chalk ground yellows more than an oil ground. Its faults would be minimised if it were to be used on board with an opaque palette, i.e. the yellowing of the ground would show less if the oil painting were opaque. Canvas mounted on board would be better than canvas on an open stretcher. Unless you specifically need this ground to paint on, the oil ground or gesso already described are quicker to make, allow much more room for error and offer a wider scope.

General recipe for half-chalk ground or emulsion

Size the canvas or board as usual. See pages 18, 21, 91. Or mount the canvas on board as for an oil ground.

Make the gesso (see *Making the gesso*, page 91) with titanium or zinc and whiting in a 1:1 proportion, e.g. 50 g (2 oz) titanium and 50 g (2 oz) whiting if using a total of 100 g (4 oz) of pigment. This is to try to offset the yellowing effect of the oil.

The oil content can be between 20–30% in liquid volume of the gesso. Some recipes use boiled oil, but this will make the ground yellow and brittle. It is used because it's quicker drying than other linseed oils. Sun-thickened linseed oil will not embrittle as much as boiled oil, will dry at approximately the same rate, but can darken like boiled oil. Stand oil will have the least yellowing effect, will remain the most flexible, but is a slow drier.

Add the oil in a slow stream to the hot gesso and stir it continuously until there are no oil droplets visible, i.e. until it emulsifies. Apply one coat as thin as possible using a wavy mottler (fig. 25) to push the ground into the weave of the canvas. A thin coat is much less likely to crack.

Leave to dry. Sun-thickened oil emulsion should be left to dry for a week, whilst stand oil emulsion may take up to three. A second coat will take 2–3 times longer to dry than the first coat and will also make the ground less flexible. If the ground is painted on before it's dry, it will crack the painting as it dries. It may also be over absorbent until it is dry. Leaving the ground to dry for 6 months would eliminate the risk of such problems.

Chapter 7
PAPER

There are many makes of artists' paper, all of high quality. Access to full information is very good through retailers. See *Bibliography* (page 172). This chapter will explain terminology and give notes on uses and using paper.

Paper is made from the interlocking of fibres, usually plant fibre (cellulose).

Artists' requirements

Artists need strong paper to withstand sustained working and to resist deterioration. There are many factors determining the strength and character of paper. Aside from the manipulations possible in the papermaking, strong paper is produced from long, acid-free fibres. Each plant produces a fibre of different length. Longer fibres make the strongest paper because they interlock better. Artists' paper should not discolour.

Acidity

Acidity in the paper causes it to distintegrate. This can happen in less than a year with newspaper. Acidity can come from the fibre or from the sizing. See *Types of fibre* (below) and *Rosin size* (page 105).

Types of fibre

Wood fibres of different lengths are mixed to produce strong paper.

Two types of paper are produced from trees: mechanical woodpulp, and woodfree.

Mechanical woodpulp paper is made simply by pulping the wood. This fibre is very acidic, which leads to the quick deterioration and yellowing of the paper. Examples are newspaper and sugar paper.

Woodfree paper is made from chemical woodpulp, the fibre has been separated and cleaned. The lignin which is the acidic and yellowing component has been removed.

Some artists' papers, including some cartridges are made from woodfree fibre. In tests it does resist decay. Prices are appealing but the range is small. Cotton linter/woodfree mixtures are about the same price and increase choice somewhat. Also paper containing some cotton linter must be better than a paper with none. When financially possible, using 100% cotton paper will leave no doubt concerning the longevity of the work.

Cotton fibre direct from the plant is used for Artists' paper. It is called cotton linter. The fibre used to come from old cotton and linen clothes or clippings, hence the term 'rag' for artists' paper. Cotton is strong and non-acidic.

Linen fibres make very strong, non-acidic paper but the cost of the raw material means it is rarely made. See *Bibliography* (page 172).

Other fibres such as manilla, esparto, glass, nylon and polyester are used in various commercial papers. They are yet to be successfully exploited for artists' paper.

Oriental fibres: There are several plant fibres used in Japan, Korea and China to make strong, non-acidic paper. Batches of paper can vary in acidity. Retailers should be consulted to establish which papers are non-acidic.

Paper production

Paper is produced in three ways.

Handmade paper is strong in all directions because the fibres are meshed absolutely at random. This gives handmade sheets their surface character and makes them very stable and probably the most hard-wearing and longest surviving. Handmade paper has four deckle edges as a result of being formed by hand on a mould and deckle.

85. *Paper with four deckle edges.*

Mould-made paper is made on a cylinder-mould machine which orientates the fibres more at random than a Fourdrinier machine (see *Machine-made*). Its strength and character is therefore somewhere between handmade and machine-made paper. It is not handmade paper.

Mould-made paper has two deckle edges, formed at the two ends of the cylinder. The other two edges are made when the sheet is cut or torn from the mould. This is not made clear by some manufacturers who describe their mould-made paper as having 'four deckle edges'. See fig. 86.

Machine-made paper is made on a Fourdrinier machine which mimics the original paper-making process but in one continuous process. The paper produced is rather characterless, is directional (the fibres run in the direction of the movement of the machine) and is markedly two-sided. The rapid and strong drainage of the pulp on the mould produces a different density of fibre on each side of the paper. These two factors make it weaker (it will tear easily in one direction) and less dimensionally stable, making it cockle when in contact with moisture.

Sizing of paper

The strength of a sheet of paper is slightly improved by sizing, but the real strength is in the structure of the interwoven fibres.

The fibres making up paper are very absorbent. Blotting paper is an extreme example. This absorbency has to be reduced or paint will sink straight in, it will look dull, the pigment will be left unbound on the paper surface, and the paint will be very difficult to work with.

Artists' paper is sized in one or both of the following ways:

Internally, a synthetic size is used in the pulp. It joins to the fibre, resulting in a paper which, even if the surface is rubbed away, will have the same absorbency all the way through. This is often needed in a heavily worked painting.

Surface-sized paper can be sized in two ways: *i.* with starch in the paper machine, which has no sizing effect, it only smooths the fibre down to improve the paper surface; and *ii.* with gelatin in the cylinder mould machine or on the dry sheet. This is called tub sizing.

The tub sizing gives an extra glow to the paint because the paint sits on the surface more, i.e. the absorbency of the paper is reduced. Water-soluble paint is also easier to remove when it is only sitting on the surface.

Tub sizing toughens the surface somewhat giving it more resilience for a heavily worked drawing.

If a paper description states the paper is surface-sized without the word gelatin, you can deduce that the surface-sizing is starch.

Unlike internal sizing, vigorous painting will remove either type of surface-sizing. Consequently surface-sized papers are also internally sized.

Buffered paper

Sometimes called calcium carbonate buffered.

Gelatin is traditionally used in conjunction with an acidic substance called alum. Alum emphasizes (hardens) the gelatin effects on the paper. Alum makes the paper acidic. This acidity is successfully counteracted by buffering the paper with an alkaline buffer, e.g. calcium carbonate. A small amount is incorporated into the paper at the pulp stage. This overpowers any acidity from the alum. Gelatin can be fixed without using any acidic substance but that process which is used by St Cuthbert's Mill (Inveresk) is not disclosed. Any buffering in that case would be only to counteract atmospheric acidity.

Rosin size

Prior to synthetic size, rosin and alum were used at the pulp stage for internal sizing. The rosin had a yellowing and embrittling effect on the paper and the alum caused acidity. This method of sizing is no longer used for artists' paper, but may still be used for other papers.

Waterleaf and soft sizing

A note for printmakers:

Papers for intaglio printmaking need to be soft so that the paper can take a true cast of the plate. A surface-sized paper interferes with this. Surface-sized paper should be soaked in warm/hot water for at least 30 minutes to dissolve the glue. A heavily sized sheet may need to be soaked for up to 12 hours. Pouring off the water and glue solution and replacing it with fresh water, hastens the process.

Soft-sized paper has a low level of internal sizing to retain the softness of the paper fibre. Waterleaf has no sizing at all for the same reason. Waterleaf gives a glowing, detailed appearance to a print because it is so soft.

Soft-sized and waterleaf papers became popular in the twentieth century when the availability of old rag watercolour paper declined. An old piece of paper (i.e. tub-sized paper, approximately 20–40 years old) gives an excellent cast of a plate because the surface-sizing has broken down, softening the paper. This cannot be mimicked by the soaking of a new sheet of surface-sized paper. As internal sizing on mould- and machine-made paper became more common, the old papers ran out and soft-sized papers have taken their place.

Because soft-sized papers are not surface-sized they do not require long soaking. A medium weight paper (250 gsm) will need only approximately 5 minutes to soften the fibre for a good cast.

Soft-sized and waterleaf papers are rather limited for painting because the paint sinks into them rather quickly, and can leave a weak film of underbound pigment on the paper surface (see page 104).

Wove and laid paper

Wove paper is formed on a woven mesh.

Laid paper made by hand or on a cylinder-mould is formed on a mesh made of wires laid over each other at right angles. Laid paper made by Fourdrinier machine is wove paper which has been embossed with a laid pattern.

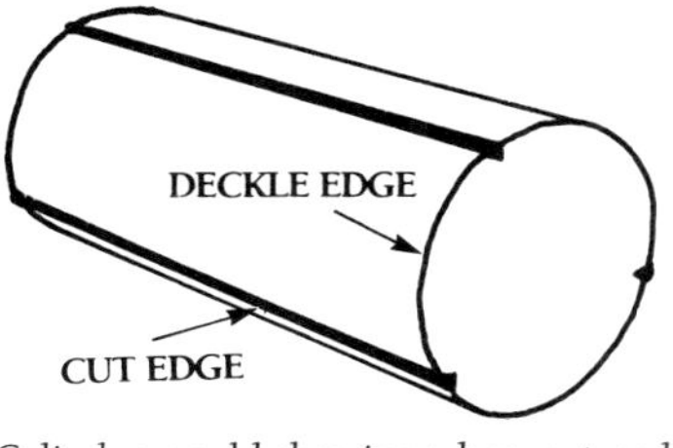

87. *Cross-section of laid mould showing more pulp on lower wires during production of laid handmade or mould-made sheet.*

86. *Cylinder mould showing where cut and deckle edges are formed (three sheets of paper).*

88. *Wove* (left) *and laid (Fourdrinier) paper.*

A watermark is made in the same way either by stitching/brazing the design on to the mould or on the Fourdrinier machine by embossing it into the wet sheet.

A greater proportion of pulp is deposited on the lower wires of the cylinder-mould. On the Fourdrinier machine the paper fibre is displaced and produces higher density lines of pulp. When either paper is pressed and dry, a lined pattern results.

There is no difference in stability between wove and laid papers.

Laid paper can be used to effect in drawings, where charcoal/pastel take more to the thicker stripes in the paper, giving a ribbed effect. Some printmaking papers are very subtly laid and can be used to good effect in a print, in either the inked or border area.

The surface of the paper

Paper is produced with three surfaces:

Rough paper reflects the rough surface of the blanket between which the formed sheet is pressed.

Not (USA: Cold-pressed) stands for not hot-pressed. It is rough paper which has been pressed again (cold) without the blanket, the pattern of the blanket being flattened.

Hot-pressed (HP) paper is Not paper which has had a hot pressing. This smooths the paper considerably by ironing down the fibres.

These surfaces are relative to each make of paper. One maker's Rough is another one's Not! etc. When choosing a paper, artists should look at all the makes in order to get the right surface for the cheapest price. See fig. 89.

Weight of papers

Papers are weighed in metric and imperial measurements. Loosely speaking, a heavy paper is thick and a light paper is thin. I say loosely speaking because a heavy, thin paper could be made by increasing the density of the pulp.

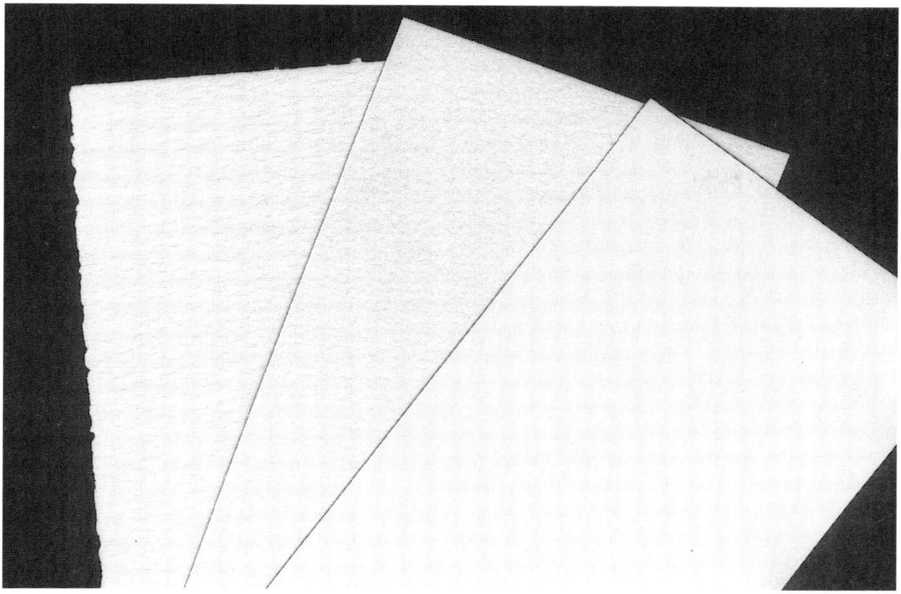

89. Left to right: *Rough, Not, and HP paper.*

If you execute a painting on paper with a sparing amount of water, it will remain reasonably flat, particularly if it is a heavy piece of paper. A handmade sheet will also tend to dry flatter than a mould-made or machine-made piece, in that order. The random orientation of fibres in a handmade sheet produces a more dimensionally stable sheet.

However, for a water-rich method or sustained painting, any paper will cockle as it absorbs water. This can be avoided by stretching the paper in the first place (see page 74). You can then also save money by using lighter weight papers.

Heavyweight papers are not categorically better than lighter ones. It is from the point of view of long term stability and age that this loose condemnation of lightweight paper stems. A heavier paper is more resistant to tearing/rough storage and is stronger simply because there is more interwoven fibre. This must be taken in context however as any cotton paper will last indefinitely if kept as recommended. See *Papers*, page 172.

The right side of the paper

The right side is that side which shows the watermark the right way round and is often smoother.

As mentioned under *Paper production*, machine-made paper is markedly two-sided. Mould-made may be perceptibly two-sided, whilst handmade paper is not. Although these technical differences exist, artists should use the side which suits the work in hand as they often offer different effects.

Chapter 8
DRAWING MATERIALS

Any of the materials mentioned in this chapter can be mixed. Some materials will not adhere well to each other, e.g. chalk pastel over wax pastel or pastel and charcoal over graphite, but you will be able to see and feel this when using those materials.

Resuming drawings

Drawings can be resumed at any time either by removing the charcoal, pastel, pencil, etc., or by adding to the original. There won't be any problems of adhesion between the old and the new.

SUPPORTS AND GROUNDS

The following drawing materials are suited to work on paper because the paper acts as a file, removing particles from the drawing tool and holding them in the interstices and the paper fibres. The paper is both the support and ground.

90. *Pigment particles in interstices of paper.*

Rag paper is recommended (see page 102).

Paper and board provide a more stable support than canvas because drawing materials lack the flexibility needed to withstand the movement of the canvas. Canvas mounted on board is a possibility. See pages 22, 46, and 89. Boards obviously offer maximum rigidity.

Gesso is also suitable for the same reason but takes longer to prepare. See page 85 for preparation of gesso boards and page 94 for sizing if necessary.

Acrylic gesso primer (it has extra tooth compared to ordinary acrylic primer) will also file off particles but is best used on board because of its flexibility compared to drawing materials.

SILVERPOINT AND OTHER METALS

Preparation of supports particular to metal drawings

Metals are too hard to be filed off by paper fibres alone. Paper needs a coating of pigment particles to catch the metal.

Stretch the paper of your choice (see page 74).

To have plain white paper, paint on a layer of white watercolour. This will be more or less imperceptible but renders the paper hard enough to pick up the metal.

White gouache or acrylic primer can be used if you want a more dominant primer/ less dominant paper surface.

A coloured watercolour or gouache can be used, if you want a coloured paper ground.

Gesso does not need to be sized for metal drawings. See pages 85, 95 for making and colouring gesso boards.

The metals

Wire can be held in a clutch pencil if it's tight enough; or just pushed into a piece of wooden dowling. However, a proprietary holder is not expensive, grips the silver well and has ends of four different sizes to hold a variety of metal thicknesses (each end can be unscrewed and reversed).

Metals produce light and airy drawings.

Silver produces a grey line which tarnishes to brown.
Gold gives a brown/grey line very similar to silver which also tarnishes.
Platinum gives a grey line which does not tarnish.
Plumber's and tinman solder (60% lead) gives a dark grey line, more dense and like pencil than the other metals. It can tarnish to a brown.

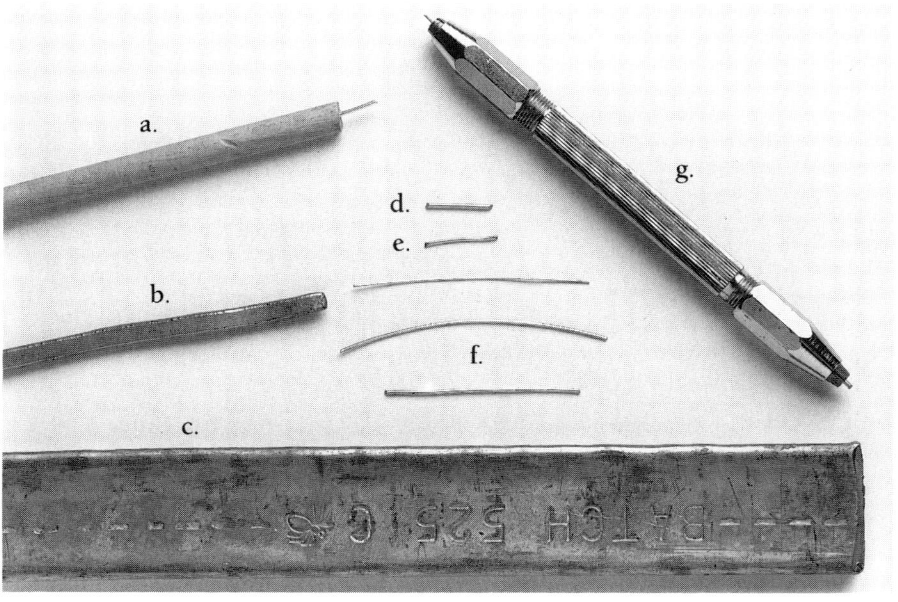

91. a. *Silver in wooden dowel;* b. *tinman solder;* c. *plumber's solder;* d. *platinum;* e. *gold;* f. *three thicknesses of silver;* g. *proprietary holder with thin and thick silver.*

Using metals

New pieces of wire can have sharp burrs at the end. Roll the new wire end on some fine emery paper to remove any sharpness which could cut the paper.

Metal marks cannot be removed from paper without removing the paper surface as well; nor can they be removed from acrylic primer.

Although gesso takes longer to prepare, its advantage for sustained metal drawings is that marks can be removed by sanding down the gesso (see page 94).

A smooth support will allow continuous lines to be drawn while the stylus on a rough support will bounce over the high spots, giving a broken line effect.

Silverpoint drawings can be useful instead of pencil or charcoal for under-drawings because it shows far less through thin paint, especially for tempera and watercolour. Gesso boards can be sized for watercolour and oil painting after the silverpoint drawing is complete. See page 94.

SCRAPERBOARD

A scraperboard is a board coated with a white ground and surfaced with black ink which can be scraped away to produce a white on black drawing.

Scraping techniques can also be used with encaustic and oil pastels. See *Bibliography* (page 172) for sources on preparing traditional scraperboards.

CHARCOAL, GRAPHITE AND VARIATIONS OF THE SAME

Preparation of supports particular to charcoal etc.

Paper does not have to have any preparation. But gelatin surface-sized paper or surfaced paper or board will allow much heavier drawing (see pages 104, 115, 93).

Gesso and acrylic primers can also be used direct. Acrylic primers can also be surfaced (see page 49).

Lead pencils are made of graphite and clay. The harder the pencil (*H*=hard) the more clay in the mixture. The softer the pencil (*B*=black) the more graphite in the mixture. *F* (firm) is between *H* and *HB*.

The same scale of hardness is also used for graphite sticks and compressed charcoal, although different companies' scales may not correlate, i.e. one company's 2B may be equivalent to another's 4B.

Graphite also comes in sticks of various sizes without wooden casing and also in soluble pencil form.

Charcoal, graphite and black pigments in general are cheap to produce and completely lightfast. Provided you choose a stable support, any of these materials, regardless of manufacturer will be quite stable. Each brand can be quite different so choose the brand which you like or which is cheapest. The photograph (fig. 92) shows a range of these materials.

Any type of eraser can be used. For complete removal of marks a white plastic rubber is excellent. See *List of sources* (page 169).

See *Fixatives* (page 117).

Oil charcoal: To give effects similar to oily crayons, charcoal can be oiled. It should be used on gelatin surface-sized paper in order to protect the paper from the oil.

Stand sticks of charcoal in a jar and fill the jar with refined linseed oil (cheapest and a suitable quality for this job). Keep the jar topped up with oil for 24 hours. Then remove the charcoal, wipe off excess oil and wrap sticks individually in aluminium foil to prevent them going hard. Oil charcoal will go hard as the oil dries and should be made and used as required.

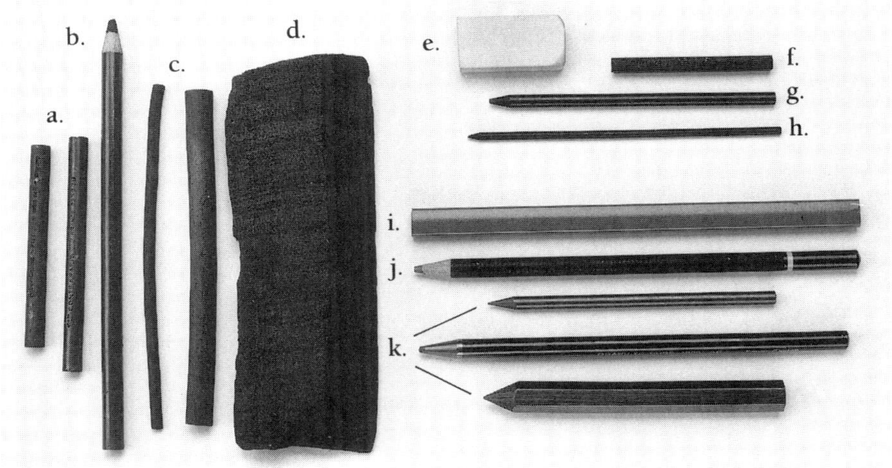

92. a. *Compressed charcoal* (Fusain); b. *charcoal pencil;* c. *medium and thick charcoal;* d. *Maimeri triangular charcoal;* e. *white eraser;* f. *conté carré;* g. *black crayon;* h. *Pierre Noir crayon;* i. *square graphite pencil;* j. *soluble graphite pencil;* k. *graphite without wooden casing.*

COLOURED PENCILS

Preparation of supports particular to coloured pencils

None of the supports need any further preparation. Paper is best stretched if a lot of solvent is to be used (see page 74). Gelatin surface-sized paper may be more stable if you use a lot of solvent for turpentine-soluble pencils.

Pencils and using them

Coloured pencils for artists come in four basic types. Charcoal/pastel, non-soluble, water-soluble and turpentine-soluble. The binder in coloured pencils is a synthetic resin.

Coloured pencils for artists are now being made with lightfast pigments rather than dyes. See *Appendix A* (page 152) for brand details.

Distilled water is recommended for use with water-soluble pencils (see page 83).

White spirit is recommended for thinning turpentine-soluble pencils because it will stain the paper less. Turpentine residue can also yellow. White spirit evaporates more quickly than turpentine, so you will have less time to move the colour around. Solvent in a spray form can be useful for wetting stretched paper. Some coloured pencils can be moved with heat, similar to encaustic. See *Oil pastels and using them*, page 119.

White plastic erasers are recommended for maximum removal of marks. See *List of Sources* (page 169).

COMMERCIAL PENS

Black pens are reasonably reliable but not all are lightfast. Commercial pens are best avoided because of the possible use of fugitive dyes. Permanent markers refer more to the waterproof binder rather than to the colour! Nibs and lightfast inks would be a better substitute for commercial pens.

NIBS, QUILLS, REED AND BAMBOO PENS

Apart from the many types of metal nibs, quills and reed pens offer unique types of marks and are worth considering.

Quills: Goose and turkey are mostly used, although crow, sea-gull and swan have been used, particularly in the past. It is probably the resilience which promotes these types of quill. Of course you can try any feather. See *Cutting a nib.*

Reed pens are made from the common reed plant, phragmites communis/phragmites Australis. The reeds are harvested in late autumn and dried before cutting a nib. Here again you can try any hollow plant stalk.

Bamboo pens are the toughest natural pens.

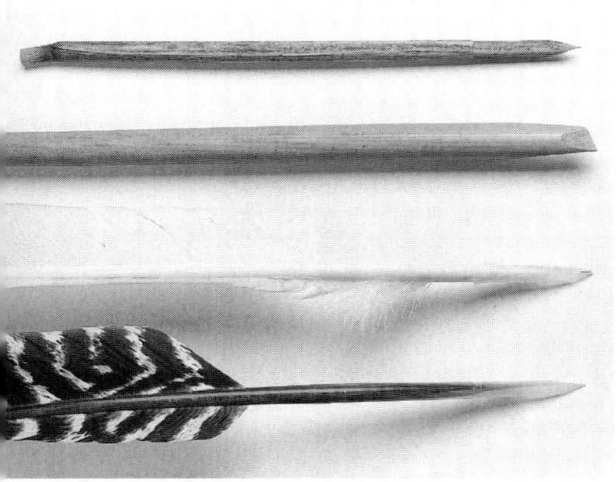

93. *Reed and bamboo pens, goose and turkey quills.*

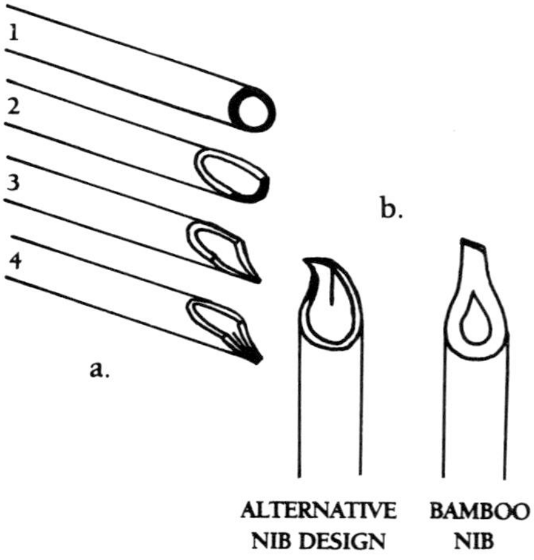

94. a. *Steps in cutting a nib.* b. *Nib designs for right-handed people.*

Cutting a nib

Nibs can be cut in any of the ways shown in fig. 94 or you can invent your own. Nibs can continue to be cut from a length of reed or bamboo as each nib wears down, until there is not enough pen left to hold.

COLOURED INKS

Preparation of supports particular to inks

Paper should be stretched (see page 74).

Gesso should be sized if you want similar control to using inks on sized paper. Unsized gesso can be rather absorbent. See gesso chapter (page 85) and *Sizing gesso* . . . (page 94).

Inks and using them

Most coloured inks are waterproof when dry but it should be stated on the bottle.

Coloured inks are bound with either shellac or acrylic. Acrylic probably remains more transparent and flexible than shellac in the long term. Coloured inks are increasingly being made with more lightfast pigments, and are generally being called liquid acrylics.

Drawing inks containing dyes should be avoided because of the fugitive nature of the dyes. 'Brilliant' watercolours are based on dyes for graphic reproduction work and are not lightfast. See *Appendix A* (page 154–5) for brand details.

Aside from the more common Indian ink (usually shellac based) black ink also comes in the form of sticks from China. This is made from pigment and natural glue. It

95. Clockwise: *Ink on Formica, Chinese ink stick, ink stone.*

is made liquid by rubbing it with water on to an ink stone or a piece of Formica.

Coloured ink sticks are probably best avoided as the pigments may not be lightfast.

Inks can be thinned with water. Distilled water is recommended (see page 83).

CHALK PASTELS

Preparation of supports particular to pastel, charcoal and graphite drawings

Paper does not have to be prepared for pastel. However, the nature of pastel, charcoal and graphite is the textural relationship between the pigment particles and the paper. This is obscured if the picture is fixed. Fixative can also darken the colour and make it more transparent. So, the more the paper grips the pastel the less it will need fixing.

Using a Rough or Not sheet of gelatin surface-sized paper rather than an HP one will help (see page 106). The pastel is held in the undulations of the paper and the gelatin surface sizing provides a surface which does not break down from vigorous work. See page 104.

96. *Cross-section of Rough and Not papers showing trapped pastel.*

For heavy work, pastel and charcoals are really improved by using a surfaced paper or board. Flour paper used in woodwork provides an ideal grip. However, the paper backing is not rag (see page 102). To obtain a surfaced rag paper you must prepare your own.

Flocked (velours) paper is paper coated with powdered cotton. The backing is not rag and the colours tend to be rather bright and not particularly lightfast. It has the same purpose and disadvantages as flour paper.

97. *Flour paper, front and back.*

Making surfaced pastel paper

This can be done by using toothed acrylic primer (see page 49).

Stretch the paper of your choice (see page 74).

Paint on a layer of toothed acrylic primer and leave to dry for 1–3 hours to make sure the surface is dry and hard. An even toothier surface can be obtained by using acrylic emulsion and approximately 30% inert pigment.

98. *Surfaced pastel paper.*

Natural glues can be used to prepare surfaced pastel paper but they can encourage mould.

Gesso can also be surfaced for drawings (see page 93).

Boards can also be toothed with acrylic primer (see page 49).

Coloured papers

Pastel is an opaque medium and does not therefore rely on a white ground. The brightness of the pastel comes from the reflection of light through the pigment itself. Coloured papers will have no effect on the stability of colour in the pastel.

However, coloured pastel papers sold for artists may be coloured with fugitive dyes or pigments. Manufacturers or retailers should be able to tell you if the papers are lightfast, or ideally the Colour Index Generic Names of the pigments used. 'Permanent' is too vague a term to be relied upon! See also *Lightfastness* (page 128). If your drawing does not cover the paper completely it will be important that your paper does not fade.

The stability of coloured papers can be assured by colouring your own rag paper. Other media on coloured paper will also be more stable if permanently coloured rag papers are used.

Colouring paper

Wet tinting: To approximate internally-coloured paper, watercolour and *Method A* should be used. Gouache can be used for a heavier effect.

Stretch the paper of your choice (see page 74).

Method A. Wet the stretched paper using a sponge or garden spray and leave for the water to soak in for a few minutes. Then paint on the colour of your choice and leave to dry. Artists' wash brushes are available and produce an even wash.

Method B. Paint the colour of your choice on to dry stretched paper and leave to dry.

Dry tinting: Internally coloured paper can also be approximated by using the dry pigment of your choice. This method does not need stretched paper in itself but if the paper is going to be painted on then stretch it before colouring it, as the pigmented paper can be blotchy after soaking. Use a dry toothbrush to rub the dry pigment well into the paper fibre. Avoid the use of any toxic pigments.

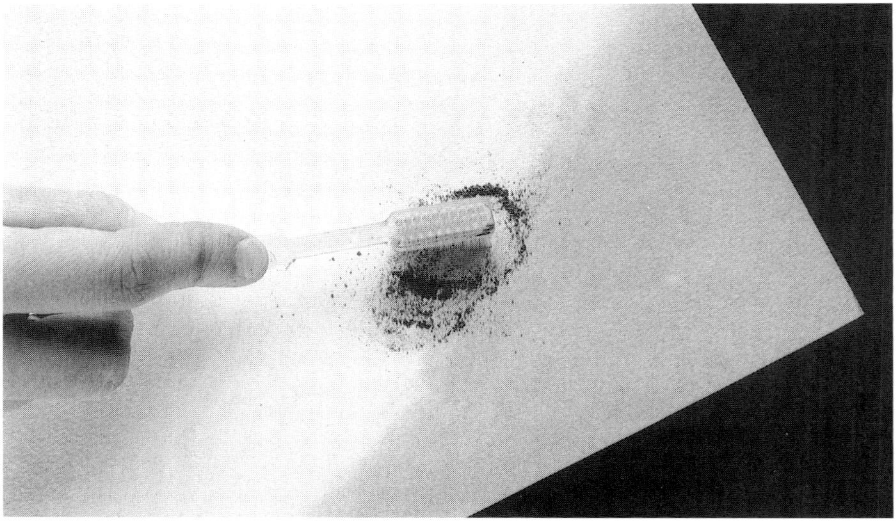

99. *Dry tinting paper with pigment.*

Coloured surfaced paper

This can be achieved by using the acrylic paint of your choice with a coarse inert pigment as in *Making surfaced pastel paper* (see page 115).

Gesso and acrylic boards can also be coloured and toothed. See pages 49, 97.

Pastels and using them

The binder for chalk pastels is usually a weak gum. Just enough to hold the pigment together.

Pigments

Permanent pigments should be used.

Note on toxicity

Toxic pigments should not be used for pastels because of their powdery nature and hence the inhalation risk. See *Toxicity* (page 129).

Where a pigment is both toxic and sensitive to atmospheric pollution it would be doubly unwise to use it in pastels because of the lack of binder and hence the lack of protection for you or the pigment.

Opaque tints of colours are made by mixing the full strength wet colour batch with more and more white, making some pastels at each stage of reduction. This is not extending the pigment. The shades are made this way and the medium is supposed to be opaque. Because of the large amounts of white pigment used in producing the paler shades of pastels, pigments whose lightfastness is reduced in half strength (quarter strength etc.) should be avoided unless used for full strength pastels, i.e. those with Blue Wool Scale numbers of 7 or 8 should be used instead.

Pastels containing high quality pigments can be expensive, especially for large ones. Pastels can be made successfully and economically in the studio. See *Appendix A* (page 156) for brand details and *Making chalk pastels* recipe (page 120).

Fixatives

Fixatives are made from synthetic resin. See *List of sources*, page 165.

As previously mentioned, fixatives negate the textural quality of pastels, darken and translucify the colours. If this doesn't bother you then there is no problem.

Fixative can be invisibly employed in between layers to enable you to work over and into areas, without the pastel/charcoal lifting up.

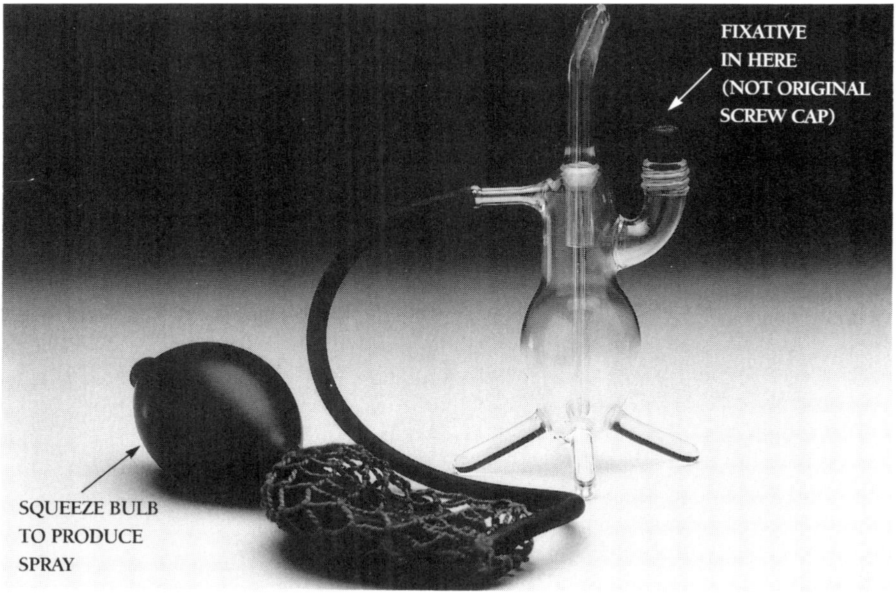

100. *Atomizer with hand pump.*

If the picture really needs a final protective layer, the finer it is, the more subtle any change will be and the more you can control the result. Three thin layers of fixative are more stable than one thick one. A fine layer can be applied using a spray gun or an atomizer (fig. 100).

You must protect your skin and eyes and wear a respirator when using a spray gun. See *Health and safety* (page 9).

An atomizer is cheaper than a gun but is more easily broken. Care should also be taken not to get liquid into the rubber hose, because the valve at the end of the rubber bulb will rust. Any build up of limescale can be removed by standing the atomizer, nozzle-end up in a glass jar with approximately 28 ml (1 fl oz) of nitric acid for 24 hours. Wear rubber gloves and protective glasses and do this outside unless you have a fume cupboard. Do not get any water in the acid. Rinse the atomizer in lots of water. See *List of sources* (page 165).

Either apparatus enables you to produce a very fine even spray. Unlike aerosols, mouth atomizers or garden sprays, there are no drips or sudden splodges, and you can fix with the picture horizontal which will prevent any fix dripping down the paper. Not that the fix should be that heavy anyway! The atomizer is used by pumping the rubber bulb with your hand.

Fixatives should be used outside because some of the solvents used are particularly **toxic**.

If you have a delicate mixed-media picture, fixing with diluted acrylic emulsion can be useful because it glues any loose particles down more successfully than fixative. Acrylic emulsion may not adhere well over oil pastels.

Dilute the emulsion with 10% water. However, the piece needs to be on stretched paper because the acrylic is water-based. Acrylic emulsion comes in matt or gloss and can be used in a spray gun or atomizer. PVA can be used but is more likely to yellow in time. Clean the gun/atomizer with water followed by a proprietary cleansing fluid. See *List of sources* (page 165). Pump both through to clean the nozzle thoroughly. Dried acrylic within the nozzle is very difficult to remove.

You can also fix with liquid acrylic inks, resulting in a layer/s of colour over and/or in between the pastel/charcoal. You can also try acrylic paint, but because of the amount of pigment in it, it may need to be diluted more than 10% (and lose some of its fixing ability) to get it through the atomizer, particularly if it is thick to start with. Clean the gun/atomizer thoroughly as suggested above. See *Coloured inks* in *Appendix A* (page 154) for liquid acrylic inks.

OIL AND WAX PASTELS

Preparation of supports particular to oil and wax pastels

Paper does not need any further preparation for these pastels. Gelatin surface-sized paper will offer maximum durability because the paper surface withstands vigorous working. Surfaced paper can be used if desired. Gesso does not need to be sized.

Canvas is not a suitable support for these pastels because they lack the necessary flexibility. Canvas can be used on board if wished. See pages 22, 46, 89.

Wax pastels

The binder for these is usually a mixture of waxes and animal fat. The very cheapest wax crayons are usually in this category. The pigments are not usually lightfast. Cheap waxes can yellow and embrittle.

See *Appendix A* (page 151) for brand details including any known information.

Oil pastels and using them

Oil pastels are in fact also bound with mixtures of waxes. Fortunately the quality of the waxes and pigments are much higher in these ranges but the prices are higher too.

Oil pastels are soluble in turpentine if desired. White spirit is recommended however as it stains the paper less. Any turpentine residue will also yellow. White spirit evaporates quicker than turpentine and you will have less time to move the colour around. Paper should be stretched if a lot of solvent is to be used.

Oil pastels can be moved with heat, similar to encaustic paint. A hair dryer or infra-red lamp will make the colours wet. Oil pastels could be combined with encaustic paint. Use pastels with lightfast pigments if you want to retain the lightfast quality of the painting. Good quality pigments in the pastels indicate as far as possible that good quality waxes have also been used. See *Appendix A* (page 151) for brand details.

Making wax pastels

101. *Wax pastel cast in individual cake tin, and empty cake tin (approx. 75 × 25 mm).*

Cold encaustic paint can be used to make wax pastels. The use of beeswax etc. and lightfast pigments offer a reliable pastel compared to the wax crayons mentioned previously. These pastels are very much harder than oil pastels.

The various binders mentioned in the encaustic chapter can be used according to the hardness/softness of pastel required. Some experimentation will be needed to get a usable pastel. Use at least 20% pigment for a well coloured pastel. See *Making the paint* (page 55) for full explanation.

Pastels are best cast in metal cake tins, preferably small individual ones (see fig. 101). Remove the hot paint from the heat and stir it to distribute the pigment evenly throughout the wax. Watch the wax as it cools for a few minutes and just as the top is setting, pour it into the tin. Leave until cold and then tap it out. If you pour the coloured wax into the tin straight from the heat it will stick to the tin and is impossible to get out when cold.

MAKING CHALK PASTELS

Making your own pastels ensures the use of permanent pigments and offers more control over the colours and shades you want. You can also save a lot of money, particularly on large pastels.

You should wear a respirator with the correct filter when handling dry pigments. See *Health and safety* (page 9).

The Binder/s

Gum tragacanth produces relatively soft pastels. The technical grade is quite good enough as a binder, the pharmaceutical grade is more expensive.

See *Alternative binders* (page 125).

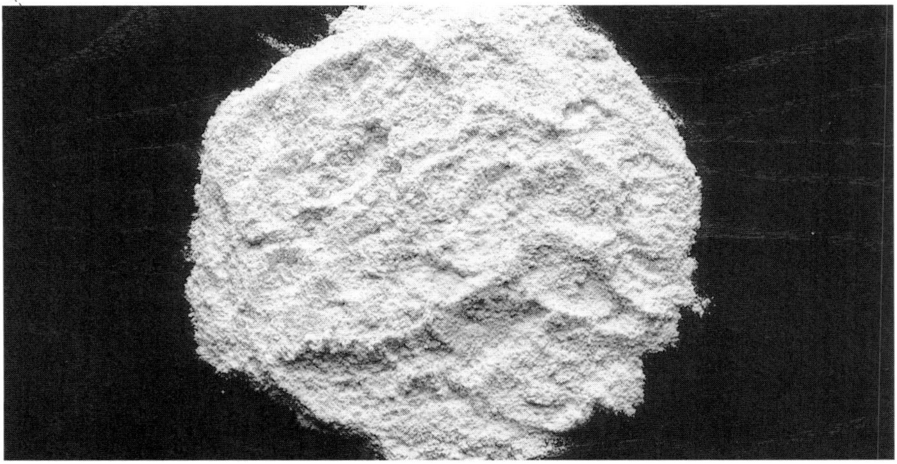

102. *Powdered gum tragacanth.*

Gum tragacanth can be kept in solution by using preservatives to discourage any mould. More importantly a preservative must be used when making your own pastels to ensure mould does not form when the pastels are used on the paper because it's very difficult to treat unbound pigment. Any unused gum solution should be kept in tightly sealed, full, sterilized bottles, and should last a year or two. You'll know if it's gone off because it will have become watery and be very smelly when you open the bottle. See page 67 for sterilizing bottles.

Soak 28 g (1 oz) of powdered gum tragacanth in 1.36 litres (48 fl oz) of cold water and stand it in a warm place overnight. The gum does not dissolve but swells. Make sure the gum doesn't stick together in lumps, or there will still be dry gum in the water in the morning. See fig. 103.

Once swollen, whisk the glue to a uniform consistency (fig. 104). Add a drop (less than one ml) of sodium benzoate preservative which is one of the safest preservatives; many others are toxic. It is bought in powder form and should be made using 1 g of powder to 99 ml ($3\frac{1}{2}$ fl oz) of water. See *List of sources* page 167. This will be *Binder A.*

103. *Swollen gum tragacanth.*

104. *Binder of uniform consistency.*

Each pigment and even different batches of the same pigment can require a different strength of binder to produce a range of pastels of similar softness. You can choose the hardness/softness of your pastels by using a stronger or weaker binder respectively. Of course you can have some soft and some hard if you want. They do need to be hard enough to hold together in stick form. Although if they are too hard the pigment won't come off on to the paper!

The other binders are made as follows.

Binder B

Mix 227 ml (8 fl oz) of *Binder A* with 227 ml (8 fl oz) water.
(1 part *A* : 1 part water)

Binder C

Mix 114 ml (4 fl oz) of *Binder A* with 341 ml (12 fl oz) water.
(1 part *A* : 3 parts water)

Binder D

Mix 85 ml (3 fl oz) of *Binder A* with 426 ml (15 fl oz) water.
(1 part *A* : 5 parts water)

Binder E

Mix 56 ml (2 fl oz) of *Binder A* with 568 ml (20 fl oz) water.
(1 part *A* : 10 parts water)

One ounce of tragacanth can result in over 200 pastels, approximately 89 × 12 mm ($3\frac{1}{2} \times \frac{1}{2}$") each, but it does depend on the pigments used.

Pigments

Pigments which have reduced lightfastness when mixed to half strength (quarter strength etc.) (see page 131) should only be made into full strength pastels. In a very pale tint of a pastel there is only a small amount of coloured pigment in relation to white pigment and any light-sensitive colour will not stand up well to daylight.

The following list gives you a starting guide for the strength of binder needed for some pigments. This is best followed up by your own notes on the strength of the binder used for each pigment, so you can reproduce the type of pastel you want.

Apart from white, pigments are noted in alphabetical order followed by the approximate binder.

Note: *A/B* means *Binder A* tending towards *Binder B*. It is suggested you start with the first binder. *E/Water* means start with *Binder E*, but you may find the pigment binds together with water alone!

White: Precipitated chalk and whiting mixed 1:1 – *A/B*

Precipitated chalk offers whiteness, pricewise it is between chalk and a coloured pigment, but on its own with tragacanth produces splintery pastels. Whiting is creamy white, is very cheap and binds the pigment better.
See page 125 for other whites.

Alizarin crimson – *B*
Alizarin/phthalocyanine blue – *C*
Burnt sienna – *D*
Burnt umber* – *B*

Cadmium red* – *A/B*
Cadmium yellow* – *B/C*
Cerulean blue – *B/C*
Chromium oxide green – *B/C*
Cobalt blue – *B*
Graphite* – *B*
Indian red – *E/water*
Ivory black – *C/D*
Light red – *E/Water*
Manganese blue* – *B*
Manganese violet* – *C/D*
Mars black – *B*
Mars red – *B*
Mars violet – *C/D*
Mars yellow – *A/B*
Phthalocyanine blue – *E/D*. Approximately 80% white needed to make first shade!
Phthalocyanine green – *E/D*. Approximately 80% white needed to make first shade!
Raw sienna – *E*
Raw umber* – *E*
Strontium yellow* – *B/C*
Ultramarine* – *B*
Viridian – *E/Water*
Viridian/cadmium yellow* – *D*
Yellow ochre – *D/E*

*The pigments marked with an asterisk in the above list are **toxic** or pollution-sensitive and ideally should be avoided in pastels.

If using a pigment which is not on the list, take a calculated guess for the strength of the binders, make test pastels and notes.

Making the pastels

The colours in pastels are mixed by making all the colours and shades you will want rather than mixing colours on a palette as in painting. This is done by first making full strength colour pastels and then making tints by successively reducing the colour batch with white. Full strength colours may be mixed before starting to produce different colours, e.g. a violet from alizarin and phthalocyanine blue.

Using the glass plate (slab) and palette knife (see fig. 45) make a small (approximately 30 × 6 mm ($1\frac{1}{4} \times \frac{1}{4}$″) white pastel by mixing a spoonful of pigment with enough *Binder A* to produce a pastry-like paste that is not too sticky (fig. 105).

Roll it out inside two sheets of newsprint (i.e. newspaper without ink on). This stops you getting your hands filthy and the absorbency of the paper also dries the pastel off a bit, making it easier to roll. Hold your fingers parallel to the pastel stick. Having the pastel stick at right angles to your fingers will produce thin uneven sausages of pastel!

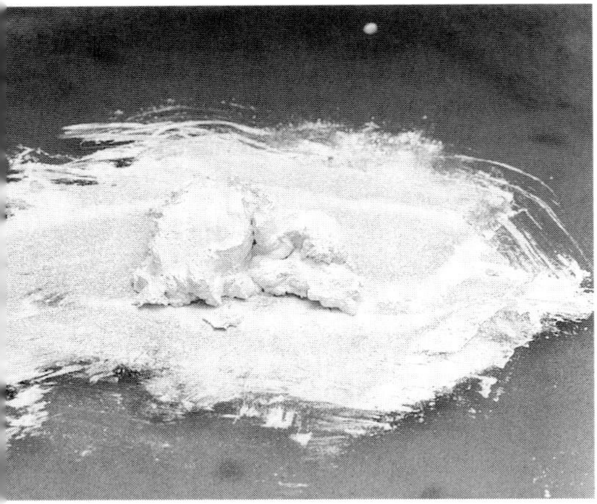

105. *White paste on plate (slab).*

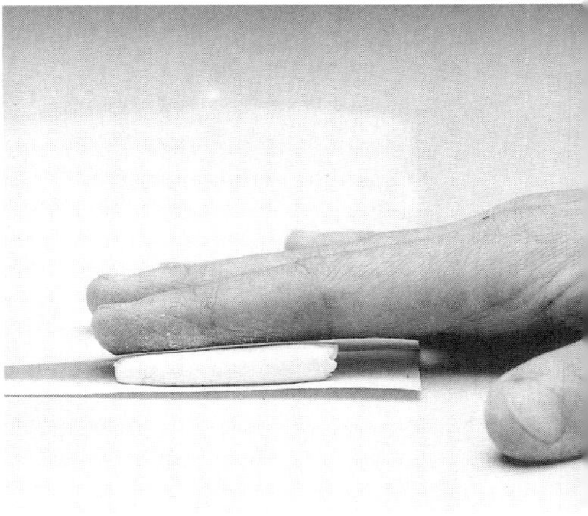

106. *Rolling pastel.*

Put the pastel in a container of some sort so you can dry it with a hairdryer without it being blown off the table! Once it is absolutely dry, approximately 5–10 minutes, test the pastel on paper for hardness/softness. If you test a half-dry pastel it will appear softer than it really is. If it's not right, make another one with stronger or weaker binder, whichever is necessary.

Once you've got it right make a good size batch of white with approximately 284 g (10 oz) of pigment. Pile the pigment on the slab, make a well in the centre and pour in the binder. Mix it to a paste consistency with the palette knife.

Choose a colour for your first pastels, e.g. yellow ochre. Make a sample pastel with it, dry and test it. Once it's okay make a batch using approximately 100 g ($3\frac{1}{2}$ oz) of pigment.

Take half the ochre paste and roll it into the size of pastel/s you want. Very large pastels, 3 cm ($1\frac{1}{4}$") diameter and more, take a long time to dry thoroughly and are therefore more likely to crack than smaller ones. This doesn't matter as long as they are usable.

To make the next tint, make up the remaining half of yellow ochre paste with at least an equal amount of white paste. You can use more or less white to get the tint you want. Some pigments are so strong that more than double of the white paste is needed in relation to the coloured paste to produce another tint sufficiently different from the last! e.g. phthalocyanines.

Mix the two pastes together on the plate (slab) until the colour is uniform, although you could have two-tone/streaky pastels if you want! Cut the paste in half, make pastels out of one half and use the second half for the next tint.

As you continue in this fashion you build up a range of the tints you want. Of course you don't have to take half the batch every time. You might make just one pastel and then make another tint or you might use all the paste up and have only one colour. Using half the batch every time is supposed to make a range which is tonally pleasing!

Leave the pastels to dry naturally. This will take between 12–48 hours.

Some pigments do not wet easily. They can be persuaded by mixing in some industrial methylated spirits (Ordinary methylated spirits may have to be used. See *List of sources*, page 167) with the pigment and binder on the plate. The alcohol evaporates off, without affecting the pastels.

Alternative binders

Any of the following gums, glues or resins can be used for binding pastels. The binders made from the standard solutions are so weak that their relative flexibilities are of less concern than they are in other media. It would seem sensible to use only one binder so that you can build up a knowledge of the strength of binder needed for the various pigments. Alternative binders could perhaps be tried with problem pigments.

Gum acacia produces harder pastels. See fig. 54.

Methyl cellulose: Wallpaper paste in the UK is no longer methyl cellulose. See *List of sources* (page 167) for retailer.

Gelatin produces crumbly pastels. See fig. 79.

Casein produces crumbly pastels. See fig. 83.

Starch glue: e.g. Arrowroot (fig. 107).

Damar varnish.

107. *Methyl cellulose* (left), *and arrowroot.*

Alternative white pigments

Using precipitated chalk and whiting 1:1 may produce a white which is rather creamy. Reduce the amount of whiting if you want the white to be whiter. The less whiting, the weaker the binder will need to be.

Talc produces a slippery texture which can be nice to work with and pastels will break less easily.
China clay produces a smoother pastel, needs a weaker binder than 1:1, whiting: precipitated chalk. Pastels break less easily, especially with Bentonite.
Titanium and **zinc** are generally not used because they overpower the coloured pigments in the paler tints.
Flake white is too **toxic** to use in its dry form.

CARE OF DRAWINGS

Drawings should be kept in portfolios or in glazed frames as they are impractical to clean and gather dirt readily. See *Appendix C* (page 160) for storing and framing work.

Varnishing

Drawings should not be varnished because of the difficulty in removing the varnish without damaging the drawing.

Chapter 9
PIGMENTS

Pigments are solids which by definition do not dissolve when mixed with a vehicle. A dye will generally only stain a vehicle. The majority of dyes when used in this way are not lightfast. Any lightfast ones are included in the pigment list (page 131).

THE CONTENTS OF THE PIGMENT LIST

Because new pigments are constantly becoming available, pigment lists quickly become outdated. However, the list given here, both by names and by Colour Index Generic Names, is as up-to-date as possible at the time of going to press.

The purpose of this list is to detail the properties of pigments used in artists' materials (i.e. not all industrial pigments) so that artists may achieve the best possible control of their media. The list gives the following information: names (including Colour Index Generic Name), lightfastness, type, opacity, and toxicity. Explanatory notes follow below.

Names

Pigments are entered under the names commonly used for artists' materials, obsolete names, some trade names and their Colour Index Generic Name.

Unfortunately the names used by manufacturers of artists' paints are not always the names used in the Colour Index International. The Colour Index Generic Name will identify which pigment is which. e.g. *Ivory black* is the common name used for artists' paints. It is entered as *Bone black* and other trade names in the Colour Index International. Its Colour Index Generic Name is C.I. Pigment Black 9.

Trade names are noted as such after their use in the list.

® after a pigment name indicates that name is a registered trade name.

Some pigments belong to 'families' of similar pigments and are cross-referenced, e.g. *Acetylene black*; See *Carbon black*.

Colour Index Generic Name

The Colour Index Generic Name refers to the standard compiled and published in the Colour Index International by the Society of Dyers and Colourists and the American Association of Textile Chemists and Colorists.

A Colour Index Generic Name is a pigment colour followed by a number, e.g. C.I. Pigment Red 83. Pigments, especially modern synthetic organic ones are best identified by this system.

Pigments which are chemically identical are grouped under one Colour Index Generic Name, even though they are different colours, e.g. *Raw Sienna* and *Burnt Sienna*, or have different handling properties, e.g. *Ivory black* and *Heavy French black*.

It must be noted that the correct terminology is, *C.I. Pigment (colour) (number)* and must be quoted as such when using it.

For the purposes of this book only, the Colour Index Generic Names in the pigment lists have been abbreviated to the following:

X = a number

C.I. Natural Black *X*	NBK *X*
C.I. Pigment Black *X*	PBK *X*
C.I. Pigment Blue *X*	PBL *X*
C.I. Natural Brown *X*	NB *X*
C.I. Pigment Brown *X*	PB *X*
C.I. Pigment Green *X*	PG *X*
C.I. Pigment Orange *X*	PO *X*
C.I. Natural Red *X*	NR *X*
C.I. Pigment Red *X*	PR *X*
C.I. Pigment Violet *X*	PV *X*
C.I. Pigment White *X*	PW *X*
C.I. Natural Yellow *X*	NY *X*
C.I. Pigment Yellow *X*	PY *X*

Lightfastness

The lightfastness of a pigment is dependent on amount and quality of light; length of exposure; extent of mixing with other colours, particularly white; amount of extender; type of binder; thickness of film; pigment particle size; amount of pigment in binder; type of support; and reaction to atmosphere and pollution.

Lightfastness of specific pigments in specific conditions is rated on the Blue Wool Scale (British Standard 1006) by numbers from 1–8. The 8 rating is excellent lightfastness. The degree of lightfastness is rapidly reduced at each move down the scale, so that 7 fades twice as fast as a number 8, 6 twice as fast as 7, etc. The Blue Wool Scale is used universally. A more specific system for artists has now been devised by the American Society for Testing and Materials (ASTM). See pages 9, 171.

The Colour Index Generic Name only identifies the chemical nature of the pigment. It does not take other variables into account. The Blue Wool Scale can only accurately be used if a pigment is tested in situ; the conditions affecting lightfastness are so variable that it is not possible for a Blue Wool Scale number to be given accurately to each pigment.

Use of the Blue Wool Scale in this book

The Blue Wool Scale numbers in this book have been compiled from a variety of sources. It *must* be noted that the BWS numbers correspond to a particular batch of a pigment, in a particular situation, and are used here only to provide a guide to lightfastness for artists. It must be accepted that lightfastness is an extremely difficult area to systematize. See *Discussion of artists' materials* and *Hopes for future materials*, page 7.

In this book, pigments with ratings of 7 or 8 are classed as absolutely lightfast for fine art materials. The term 'permanent' as part of a manufacturer's name does not necessarily correspond to a 7 or 8 on the Blue Wool Scale. One company's 'permanent' may be 6, whilst another's is 8!

Where pigments are significantly less lightfast when mixed with other colours, especially white, a second BWS number is given with the words 'In tint', e.g. a coloured pigment reduced with a percentage of white pigment. Try to use these colours at full strength only.

In some cases where a colour cannot be replaced, lower ratings will have to be accepted – *Aureolin* for example. Pigments rated as 5 and below should be avoided if possible.

Note: Where no Blue Wool Scale number can be found, any known information will be stated. 'Permanent' is stated where the standard of lightfastness of a pigment corresponds to a pigment which is known to be 7 or 8 on the Blue Wool Scale even though there has been no BWS number published for the 'permanent' pigment.

Type

There are three types of pigment:

i. **Inorganic**, including three groups: earth, mineral and synthetic.

ii. **Natural organic.**

iii. **Synthetic organic**, including three groups: pure organic pigments, lakes and toners.

Opacity

The opacity of a pigment can vary according to the processing of the pigment particles.

Pigments are noted in this book as transparent, opaque, somewhere in between, or of variable opacity. Paint manufacturers and/or pigment retailers should know the opacity of their products.

A transparent colour allows previous paint layers to show through whilst an opaque colour covers up previous layers, e.g. a violet can be obtained by placing a transparent red over a transparent blue, or vice versa.

Opaque pigments will appear more/almost transparent when used thinly, especially in watercolour or tempera.

Toxicity

There are three ways dry pigments affect us: *i.* Through the skin; *ii.* by inhalation; *iii.* by ingestion. The pigment content in paint can affect us by absorption through the skin and by ingestion. All pigments are potential irritants in dry form. Some pigments can have fatal effects. Where known, these are noted as ***Toxic***. The toxicity of some synthetic organic pigments is suspected but not known. *Artist Beware* by Michael McCann is strongly recommended as a reference source for the dangers of pigments. See *Bibliography* page 172.

Pigments which are incorporated in a paint binder can be safely used. Pigments in pastel form remain very dusty, hence toxic pigments should not be used in pastels. Very toxic pigments should be avoided in dry form altogether. A respirator with the correct filter should be worn when handling dry pigments. See *Health and safety* (page 9).

Additional notes are given in the list under individual pigments, e.g. a hidden lack of lightfastness, special uses or characteristics of pigment.

Inert pigments

Extenders, stabilizers and pigments used for grounds are listed in the same way as the other pigments, followed by their most common uses. They can be called inert pigments because they are inactive in artists' paint and do not retain their white colour in all media, compared to the white pigments, *flake*, *titanium dioxide* and *zinc oxide*. Some can remain white in water-based media but become transparent in oil.

The names of these pigments are grouped here for reference, the individual entries include their other names: *Alumina hydrate, barium sulphate, blanc fixe, China clay, gypsum, magnesium calcium carbonate, marble dust, mica, plaster of Paris, precipitated chalk, pumice, silica, talc, whiting.*

HOW TO USE THE PIGMENT LIST

A colour like *Cobalt blue* can simply be looked up in the alphabetical list. If you want to check, however, that a manufacturer is using *Cobalt blue* pigment and not just that name, then obtain the Colour Index Generic Name from their catalgoue or from the company if they are not yet publishing Colour Index Generic Names. You can then either obtain the pigment name from the *Pigments by numbers* list (page 142), e.g. *Pigment Blue 28* (abbreviated to PBL28 in this book) is *Cobalt Blue*; or if the manufacturers say they use *Pigment Blue 15* you can look up PBL15 and obtain its pigment name. This can then be looked up in the alphabetical list. However, many pigments have more than one name, i.e. you may be checking to see if *Thenard's blue* in a certain brand is PBL28. Therefore when you find PBL28 is *Cobalt blue* in the *Pigments by numbers* list you will have to look up *Cobalt blue* in the alphabetical list to see if *Thenard's blue* is another name for PBL28.

Some colours, like *Indian yellow, Indigo* or *Sepia*, were originally natural pigments which are fugitive and should be replaced by the manufacturers with more lightfast pigments. Colours like *Hooker's, Olive* or *Sap green* are mixtures of pigments popular in the past but which were commonly fugitive. These, too, should be replaced by a mixture of more lightfast pigments. You can check the lightfastness and other characteristics of these colours in the same way as for *Cobalt blue* above, i.e. obtain the Colour Index Generic Names for the pigments used, look them up in the *Pigments by numbers* list, then look them up by name in the alphabetical list to ascertain the lightfastness etc. of the pigments being used. Each brand you use will have to be checked, because different manufacturers probably use different pigments for their own *Indian yellow* etc.

Sometimes manufacturers use names which are not in the alphabetical list, e.g. *Purple Lake*. Again the Colour Index Generic Names should be obtained and the *Pigments by numbers* list followed by the alphabetical list should be employed to establish the qualities of the pigments being used.

THE PIGMENT LIST

See page 128 for abbreviations of Colour Index Generic Names.

ACETYLENE BLACK See CARBON BLACK.

ALIZARIN BROWN Also BROWN MADDER. Mixture of pigments. Check the Colour Index Generic Names.

ALIZARIN CRIMSON Also MADDER LAKE. PR 83. BWS 67. In tint BWS 5. Synthetic organic lake. Transparent.

ALIZARIN VIOLET PV5. BWS 6. In tint BWS 4–5. Synthetic organic lake. Transparent.

ALUMINA See ALUMINIUM HYDRATE.

ALUMINIUM HYDRATE Also ALUMINA, ALUMINIUM HYDROXIDE, ALUMINA WHITE. PW24. Permanent. Inorganic synthetic. Inert pigment. Transparent in oils. Used as extender and stabilizer and for smoothness in paints.

ALUMINIUM HYDROXIDE See ALUMINIUM HYDRATE.

ALUMINA WHITE See ALUMINIUM HYDRATE.

ANILINE BLACK PBK1. BWS 7–8. In tint BWS 6. Synthetic organic. Transparent.

ANILINE COLOURS Obsolete term for synthetic organic pigments.

ANTHRAQUINONE BLUE Also INDANTHRONE BLUE. PBL60. BWS 7–8. Synthetic organic. Transparent.

ANTHRAQUINONE RED PR177. BWS 7–8. Also PR194. BWS 8. Synthetic organic. Transparent.

ANTHRAQUINONE VIOLET PV40. BWS 7–8. Synthetic organic. Transparent.

ANTHRAQUINONE YELLOW See FLAVANTHRONE YELLOW.

ANTIMONY WHITE PW11. Permanent. Inorganic synthetic. Opaque. ***Toxic***.

ANTIMONY YELLOW See NAPLES YELLOW.

ANTWERP BLUE See PRUSSIAN BLUE.

ANTWERP RED PR101 or PR102. See MARS RED or RED OCHRE.

ARYLAMIDE YELLOWS See HANSA® YELLOW.

ASBESTINE See TALC.

ASPHALTUM Also BITUMEN. NBK6. Natural organic. Fugitive colour derived from tar. Very destructive in paint films, causing wide splits and blisters etc. in oil paint. Should be replaced by a mixture of permanent colours.

AUREOLIN Also COBALT YELLOW. PY40. BWS 7. Inorganic synthetic. Transparent.

AZO CONDENSATION (name of group of pigments)

BROWN PB23. BWS 7–8. Synthetic organic. Transparent.

RED PR166. BWS 7–8. Synthetic organic. Opaque. Also PR144. BWS 7–8. Semi-transparent.

YELLOW PY128. BWS 7–8. Synthetic organic. Transparent.

BARITE See BARIUM SULPHATE.

BARIUM CHROMATE See BARIUM YELLOW.

BARIUM SULPHATE Also BARITE, BARYTES. PW22. Unaffected by light. Mineral. Inert pigment. Transparent in oil. Used as extender in paints, tooth in grounds (especially PW22) and for opacity in gouache.

BARIUM WHITE See BLANC FIXE.

BARIUM YELLOW Also BARIUM CHROMATE, LEMON YELLOW. PY31. BWS 8. Inorganic synthetic. Opaque. ***Toxic***.

BARYTES See BARIUM SULPHATE and BLANC FIXE.

BASIC DYE TONER (name of group of pigments)

BLUE PBL1. BWS 6–4. Synthetic organic. Transparent.

GREEN PG1. PG2. BWS 6–4. Reduced in tint. Synthetic organic. Transparent.

RED PR81. BWS 6–4. PR82 is similar. PR90. BWS 3. / PR169. BWS 5. Reduced in tint / PR173. BWS 5. Synthetic organic. Transparent.

VIOLET PV1. BWS 6–4. PV2, PV3. BWS 4. Synthetic organic. Transparent.

BENTONITE White American Clay. See CHINA CLAY.

BENZIDINE ORANGE See PYRAZOLONE ORANGE.

BENZIDINE YELLOW See DIARYLIDE YELLOW.

BENZIMIDAZOLONE ORANGE PO36. BWS 6–8. Also PO62, which is more lightfast. Synthetic organic. Opaque.

BENZIMIDAZOLONE YELLOW PY151, PY154, PY156. BWS 8. Synthetic organic. Variable opacity.

BERLIN BLUE See PRUSSIAN BLUE.

BETA NAPHTHOL PR6. BWS 6. In tint BWS 6–4. Synthetic organic. Opaque.

BISTRE NB11. Not permanent. Natural organic. Should be replaced by a mixture of permanent colours. RAW UMBER is a good match.

BITUMEN See ASPHALTUM.

BLACK IRON OXIDE See MARS BLACK.

BLANC FIXE Also BARIUM WHITE and BARYTES. Artificial Barium sulphate. PW21. Unaffected by light. Inorganic synthetic. Inert pigment. Transparent in oil. For uses see BARIUM SULPHATE.

BLUE BLACK See VINE BLACK.

BOLE See RED BOLE and WHITE BOLE.

BON ARYLAMIDE See NAPHTOL® AS and NAPHTHOL RED.

BONE BLACK See IVORY BLACK.

BROMINATED ANTHRANTHRONE See DIBROMANTHRONE.

BRONZE BLUE See PRUSSIAN BLUE.

BROWN IRON OXIDES See MARS BROWN.

BROWN MADDER See ALIZARIN BROWN.

BROWN OCHRE Type of YELLOW OCHRE.

BURNT GREEN EARTH Also TRANSPARENT BROWN, VERONA BROWN. PG23. BWS 7–8. Earth. Transparent.

BURNT GYPSUM See PLASTER OF PARIS.

BURNT OCHRE PB7. Also PR102. BWS 8. Earth. Variable opacity.

BURNT SIENNA Also RAW SIENNA. PR102. BWS 8. Earth. Transparent. Best grades come from Italy.

BURNT UMBER Also RAW UMBER. PB7. Also PR102. BWS 8. Earth. Transparent. ***Toxic***. Used to be used in toned oil grounds. Best grades come from Cyprus, called TURKEY UMBER. Good grades from Italy.

CADMIUM GREEN PG14. Mixture of CADMIUM YELLOW and COBALT BLUE.

CADMIUM ORANGES, REDS and YELLOWS PO20. PR108. PR113. PY35. PY37. BWS 7. Inorganic synthetic. Opaque. ***Toxic***.

CALCIUM CARBONATE See WHITING.

CAPUT MORTUUM See MARS RED.

CARBAZOLE VIOLET See DIOXAZINE VIOLET.

CARBON BLACK Also ACETYLENE BLACK, FRANKFORT BLACK, LAMP BLACK, VEGETABLE BLACK. PBK6/7. BWS 8. Inorganic. Opaque. Can be ***toxic***.

CARMINE Also SCARLET LAKE. NR4. Not permanent. Natural organic. Transparent. ALIZARIN is more permanent.

CASSEL EARTH See VANDYKE BROWN.

CERULEAN BLUE Trade name, COERULEUM. PBL35. BWS 7. Synthetic inorganic. Opaque.

CERUSE See FLAKE WHITE.

CHALK See PRECIPITATED CHALK and WHITING.

CHARCOAL BLACK See VINE BLACK.

CHINA CLAY Also BENTONITE, BOLE, KAOLIN, WHITE BOLE. PW19. Mineral. Semi-transparent. ***Toxic***. Inert pigment. Transparent in oil. Sometimes used as a stabilizer or thickener in paints, for white in pastels and can be used in gesso.

CHINESE WHITE See ZINC WHITE.

CHLORINATED PARA RED PR4. BWS 6. In tint BWS 4. Synthetic organic. Semi-opaque.

CHROME GREEN Also MILORI GREEN. Mixture of CHROME YELLOW and PRUSSIAN BLUE. PG15. BWS 6–7. Best replaced by CADMIUM/PHTHALOCYANINE mixture. ***Toxic***.

CHROME ORANGE See CHROME YELLOWS and ORANGES.

CHROME YELLOWS and ORANGES Also LEAD CHROME, PARIS YELLOW. PY34. PO21. BWS 6–8. Inorganic synthetic. Opaque ***Toxic***. Tend to brown and darken from atmospheric pollution.

CHROMIUM OXIDE GREEN Also OXIDE OF CHROMIUM. PG17. BWS 8. Inorganic synthetic. Opaque.

CINNABAR Obsolete mineral. Not permanent. Replaced by VERMILION. ***Toxic***.

COBALT BLUE Also KING'S BLUE, THENARD'S BLUE. PBL28. BWS 7–8. Inorganic synthetic. Semi-transparent. Dry oil film can look dull and cloudy, but original colour is restored when painting is varnished.

COBALT GREEN PG19. BWS 7–8. Inorganic synthetic. Opaque.

COBALT TITANATE GREEN See LIGHT GREEN OXIDE.

COBALT TURQUOISE Also TURKISH GREEN. PBL36. BWS 7–8. Inorganic synthetic. Semi-transparent.

COBALT VIOLET PV14. BWS 7–8. Inorganic synthetic. Semi-opaque.

COBALT YELLOW See AUREOLIN.

COERULEUM See CERULEAN.

COLOGNE EARTH See VANDYKE BROWN.

CREMNITZ WHITE See FLAKE WHITE.

CYAN Certain shade of blue used for four-colour printing. Check Colour Index Generic Names as this colour is often used for work which is reproduced and then thrown away. May be PBL15:3.

DAVY'S GREY PBK19. BWS 8. Mineral. Semi-transparent. ***Toxic***.

DIARYLIDE ORANGE See PYRAZOLONE ORANGE.

DIARYLIDE YELLOW ALSO BENZIDINE YELLOW. PY12, PY14. BWS 4. In tint BWS 4–2. / PY13, PY17. BWS 5–6. / PY16. BWS 5. / PY83. BWS 6. In tint BWS 6–4. / Opaque PY83 has improved lightfastness. Synthetic organic. Variable opacity.

DIBROMANTHRONE Also BROMINATED ANTHRANTHRONE. PR168. BWS 8. Synthetic organic. Semi-transparent.

DINITRANILINE ORANGE Also HANSA® ORANGE and HANSA® RED. PO5. BWS 7. In tint BWS 5. Synthetic organic. Variable opacity.

DIOXAZINE PURPLE See DIOXAZINE VIOLET.

DIOXAZINE VIOLET Also CARBAZOLE VIOLET, DIOXAZINE PURPLE. PV23. BWS 7–8. Synthetic organic. Transparent.

DOLOMITE See MAGNESIUM CALCIUM CARBONATE.

DRAGON'S BLOOD NR31. Not permanent. Natural organic resin. ALIZARIN is more permanent.

DROP BLACK See IVORY BLACK.

EMERALD GREEN Also PARIS GREEN. PG21. Not permanent. Inorganic synthetic. Semi-opaque. ***Toxic***. Used as an insecticide! Should be replaced by a mixture of permanent colours. PHTHALOCYANINE GREEN and HANSA® YELLOW are a good match.

ENGLISH RED See RED OCHRE.

FERROUS NITROSO-BETA NAPHTHOL LAKE PG12. BWS 6. In tint BWS 4–5. Synthetic organic. Transparent.

FLAKE WHITE Also CERUSE, CREMNITZ WHITE, LEAD WHITE, WHITE LEAD. PW1. BWS 7. Inorganic synthetic. Opaque. *Toxic*. Tends to yellow in oil. May brown and darken from atmospheric pollution; somewhat protected in oil, especially if painting is varnished. Colour can be reinstated by cleaning.

FLAVANTHRONE YELLOW An ANTHRAQUINONE YELLOW. Formerly PY112 now PY24. BWS 6. Darkens in full strength! BWS 7–8 in very pale tints. Synthetic organic. Transparent.

FRANKFORT BLACK See LAMP BLACK.

FRENCH CHALK See TALC.

FRENCH ULTRAMARINE See ULTRAMARINE BLUE.

GAMBOGE NY24. Not permanent. Natural organic. Transparent. Should be replaced by a mixture of permanent colours. AUREOLIN is a good match and more permanent.

GENUINE ULTRAMARINE See LAPIS LAZULI.

GERMAN BLACK See VINE BLACK.

GILDERS' WHITING See WHITING.

GOLDEN OCHRE See MARS YELLOW. Should be genuine type of ochre or synthetic iron oxide, not a mixture containing chromes.

GRAPE BLACK See VINE BLACK.

GRAPHITE Also PLUMBAGO. PBK10. Permanent. Mineral. Opaque. *Toxic*.

GREEN EARTH Also TERRE VERTE, VERONA GREEN. PG23. BWS 7–8. Earth. Transparent.

GREEN GOLD See NICKEL AZO YELLOW.

GUIGNET'S GREEN See VIRIDIAN.

GYPSUM PW25. Mineral. Semi-opaque. Inert pigment. Can be used for gesso or in white for pastels.

HANSA is a trade name of Hoechst.

HANSA® ORANGE See DINITRANILINE ORANGE.

HANSA® RED See DINITRANILINE ORANGE and TOLUIDINE RED.

HANSA® SCARLET See TOLUIDINE RED.

HANSA® YELLOW Also ARYLAMIDE YELLOW G, GX and 10G, HANSA® YELLOW G, GX and 10G. PY1. BWS 8. In tint BWS 4. / PY3, PY98. BWS 8. In tint BWS 6–4. / PY4, PY5, PY10, PY73, PY74. BWS 8. In tint BWS 6. / PY97. BWS 8. / PY98. BWS 6–4. Synthetic organic. Variable opacity.

HEAVY FRENCH BLACK See IVORY BLACK.

HELIO is a trade name of Bayer.

HELIO FAST YELLOW 6GL ® PY23. BWS 6. Darkens in full strength! BWS 7–8 in very pale tints. Synthetic organic. Transparent.

HOOKER'S GREEN Can be a mixture of impermanent pigments. Check Colour Index Generic Names to ensure a mixture of permanent colours.

HORTENSIA BLUE See PHTHALOCYANINE BLUE.

HYDRATED CHROMIUM OXIDE See VIRIDIAN.

INDANTHRONE BLUE See ANTHRAQUINONE BLUE.

INDIAN RED See MARS RED.

INDIAN YELLOW (imitation) See NICKEL AZO YELLOW. May be made from other synthetic organic pigments of less permanency, check Colour Index Generic Names.

INDIGO NBL1. Not permanent. Natural organic. Should be replaced by a mixture of permanent colours. PHTHALOCYANINE BLUE, ULTRAMARINE and a BLACK are a good match. Check Colour Index Generic Names.

IRON BLUE See PRUSSIAN BLUE.

IRON OXIDE BLACK See MARS BLACK.

ISOINDOLINONE ORANGE PO66. BWS 7–8. Synthetic organic. Opaque.

ISOINDOLINONE YELLOW Also TETRACHLOROISOINDOLINONE. PY109, PY100. BWS 7–8. Semi-transparent. / PY137, PY139. BWS 7–8. Opaque. Synthetic organic.

IVORY BLACK Also BONE BLACK, DROP BLACK, HEAVY FRENCH BLACK. PBK9. BWS 8. Inorganic. Transparent.

KAOLIN See CHINA CLAY.

KING'S BLUE See COBALT BLUE.

LAKE RED C PR53:1. BWS 3. In tint BWS 1. Synthetic organic. Variable opacity. ***Toxic.***

LAMP BLACK See CARBON BLACK.

LAPIS LAZULI Also GENUINE ULTRAMARINE. PBL29. Mineral. Semi-transparent. Matched by ULTRAMARINE BLUE. Very expensive. May darken from atmospheric pollution. Replaced by ULTRAMARINE BLUE.

LEAD ANTIMONIATE See NAPLES YELLOW.

LEAD CHROME See CHROME YELLOWS and ORANGES.

LEAD SULPHATE PW3. BWS 7–8. Inorganic synthetic. Semi-opaque. ***Toxic.*** Used in conjunction with chrome yellow.

LEAD WHITE See FLAKE WHITE.

LEMON YELLOW See BARIUM YELLOW.

LIGHT GREEN OXIDE: Also COBALT TITANATE GREEN. PG50. BWS 8. Inorganic synthetic. Opaque.

LIGHT RED PR101or PR102. See MARS RED or RED OCHRE.

LITHOL is a registered trademark of Bayer.

LITHOL® RED PR49. BWS 5. Synthetic organic. Semi-opaque.

LITHOL® RED GG PR52:2. BWS 7, reduced in tint. Synthetic organic. Transparent.

LITHOL® RUBINE PR57:1. BWS 5, reduced in tint. Synthetic organic. Transparent. May be Magenta in four-colour printing.

LITHOPONE PW5. BWS 8. Inorganic synthetic. Transparent. ***Toxic.*** Opaque in watercolour. Used in grounds and as an extender in paints.

LUSTRE See PEARL LUSTRE.

MADDER LAKE See ALIZARIN CRIMSON and ROSE MADDER.

MAGENTA Certain shade of pink used in four-colour printing. Check Colour Index Generic Names as this colour is often used for work that is reproduced and then thrown away. See LITHOL RUBINE.

MAGNESIUM CALCIUM CARBONATE Also DOLOMITE, MAGNESIUM CARBONATE. Type of Whiting (PW18). ***Toxic***. Inert pigment. Sometimes used as extender in paints rather than whiting and could be used in gesso.

MAGNESIUM CARBONATE See MAGNESIUM CALCIUM CARBONATE.

MALACHITE Inorganic. Not permanent. Should be replaced by a mixture of permanent colours.

MANGANESE BLACK PBK14. Permanent. Inorganic synthetic. ***Toxic***.

MANGANESE BLUE PBL33. BWS 7. Inorganic synthetic. Transparent. ***Toxic***.

MANGANESE BROWN PB8. BWS 7–6. Inorganic synthetic. ***Toxic***.

MANGANESE VIOLET Also MINERAL VIOLET. PV16. BWS 7. Inorganic synthetic. Semi-transparent. ***Toxic***.

MARBLE DUST PW18. Permanent. Mineral. ***Toxic***. Inert pigment. Good tooth and whitener for grounds, including surfaced pastel paper.

MARS BLACK Also BLACK IRON OXIDE, IRON OXIDE BLACK. PBK11. BWS 8. Inorganic synthetic. Semi-opaque.

MARS BROWN Also BROWN IRON OXIDES. PB6. BWS 8. Inorganic synthetic. Semi-opaque.

MARS COLOURS Also SYNTHETIC IRON OXIDES. Used in acrylic paint rather than natural iron oxides and earths because of their greater purity. See individual MARS entries.

MARS RED Also CAPUT MORTUUM, INDIAN RED, MARS VIOLET, RED IRON OXIDE, VENETIAN RED. PR101. BWS 8. Inorganic synthetic. Variable opacity. RED OCHRE is very similar.

MARS VIOLET See MARS RED.

MARS YELLOW Also GOLDEN OCHRE, TRANSPARENT OCHRE, YELLOW IRON OXIDE. PY42. BWS 8. Inorganic synthetic. Transparent. YELLOW OCHRE is very similar.

MICA PW20. Unaffected by light. Mineral. ***Toxic***. Used to import lustre.

MILORI BLUE See PRUSSIAN BLUE.

MILORI GREEN See CHROME GREEN.

MINERAL BLUE See PRUSSIAN BLUE.

MINERAL VIOLET See MANGANESE VIOLET.

MOLYBDATE ORANGE PR104. BWS 6–7. Inorganic synthetic. Opaque. ***Toxic***. Tends to darken from atmospheric pollution.

MONA BLUE See PHTHALOCYANINE BLUE.

MONA GREEN See PHTHALOCYANINE GREEN.

MONASTRAL® is a trade name of ICI in UK and Ciba-Geigy in USA.

MONASTRAL® BLUE See PHTHALOCYANINE BLUE.

MONASTRAL® GREEN See PHTHALOCYANINE GREEN.

MONESTIAL BLUE See PHTHALOCYANINE BLUE.

MONESTIAL GREEN See PHTHALOCYANINE GREEN.

NAPHTHOL GREEN PG8. BWS 7–8. In tint BWS 5–6. Synthetic organic. Opaque.

NAPHTHOL RED Chemical name for NAPHTOL® AS.

NAPHTOL is a trade name of Hoechst.

NAPHTOL® AS Also BON ARYLAMIDE, NAPHTOL CRIMSON, NAPHTOL RED. PR2, PR12, PR170. BWS 6. / PR5, PR9, PR22, PR188. BWS 7. / PR7. BWS 4–5. / PR8, PR23, PR146. BWS 5–6. / PR112. BWS 7–8. / PR147. BWS 4. All colours reduced in lightfastness in tint. Synthetic organic. Variable opacity.

NAPHTOL CRIMSON See NAPHTOL® AS.

NAPHTOL RED See NAPHTOL® AS.

NAPLES YELLOW Also ANTIMONY YELLOW, LEAD ANTIMONIATE. PY41. BWS 7–8. Inorganic synthetic. Opaque. ***Toxic***. May brown and darken from atmospheric pollution but can be cleaned.

NATURAL IRON OXIDES See RED OCHRE and YELLOW OCHRE.

NICKEL AZO YELLOW Also GREEN GOLD and INDIAN YELLOW. PG10. BWS 7–8. Synthetic organic. Semi-transparent.

NICKEL TITANATE Also TITANIUM YELLOW. PY53. BWS 8. Inorganic synthetic. Opaque.

OCHRE See RED OCHRE and YELLOW OCHRE.

OLIVE GREEN Can be a mixture of impermanent pigments. Check Colour Index Generic Names to ensure a mixture of permanent colours.

OXIDE OF CHROMIUM See CHROMIUM OXIDE GREEN.

PARA RED PR1. BWS 6. In tint BWS 2. Synthetic organic. Opaque.

PARIS BLUE See PRUSSIAN BLUE.

PARIS GREEN See EMERALD GREEN.

PARIS WHITE See WHITING.

PARIS YELLOW See CHROME YELLOWS and ORANGES.

PAYNES GRAY Mixture of ULTRAMARINE, a BLACK and OCHRE.

PEACH BLACK Mixture of ANILINE BLACK, CARBON BLACK and IVORY BLACK.

PEARL LUSTRE Also LUSTRE. Colours with mother-of-pearl lustre. Can be from the addition of MICA. No Colour Index Generic Names. Lightfastness should be checked with manufacturer.

PERINONE ORANGE PO43. BWS 7–8. Synthetic organic. Semi-opaque.

PERSIAN RED See RED OCHRE.

PERYLENE RED (name of a group of pigments) PR190. BWS 7–8. PR179 and PR224 are similar. Synthetic organic. Transparent.

PHTHALOCYANINE BLUE Also MONASTRAL®, MONA, and MONESTIAL BLUE, HORTENSIA BLUE, often manufacturer's name e.g. Winsor blue. PBL15, PBL16. BWS 8. Synthetic organic. Transparent. PBL15:3 can be Cyan in four-colour printing.

PHTHALOCYANINE GREEN Also MONASTRAL®, MONA, and MONESTIAL GREEN, often manufacturer's name e.g. Winsor green. PG7, PG36. BWS 8. Synthetic organic. Transparent.

PLUMBAGO See GRAPHITE.

PLASTER OF PARIS Also BURNT GYPSUM. Mineral. Inert pigment. When slaked can be used in gesso.

PMA VIOLET PV39. BWS 5, reduced in tint. Synthetic organic. Transparent.

PRECIPITATED CHALK Also CHALK. PW18. Mineral. Inert pigment. Finer quality chalk than whiting. Used in white for pastels, opacity for gouache and can be used in gesso. Muddy in oil.

PRUSSIAN BLUE Also BERLIN BLUE, BRONZE BLUE, IRON BLUE, MILORI BLUE, MINERAL BLUE, PARIS BLUE. ANTWERP BLUE is a less pure form. PBL27. BWS 7. Inorganic synthetic. Transparent. Can fade in daylight but regain its colour in darkness! Replaced by PHTHALOCYANINE BLUE.

PTMA (name of group of pigments)

VIOLET PV4. BWS 2. Synthetic organic. Semi-transparent.

PUMICE PW20 and PW26. Unaffected by light. Inorganic. ***Toxic***. Powdered volcanic rock. Inert pigment. Good tooth for grounds, including surfaced pastel paper. Grey in colour.

PYRAZOLONE ORANGE Also BENZIDINE ORANGE, DIARYLIDE ORANGE. PO13. BWS 6. Transparent. / PO34. BWS 8–6. In tint BWS 4. Variable opacity. / Opaque PO34 has much improved lightfastness. Synthetic organic.

QUINACRIDONE MAGENTA Also QUINACRIDONE PINK. PR122. BWS 7–6. Synthetic organic. Semi-transparent.

QUINACRIDONE PINK See QUINACRIDONE MAGENTA.

QUINACRIDONE RED PR206, 207, 209. BWS 8. Synthetic organic. Transparent. Also PV19. BWS 8. Semi-transparent.

QUINACRIDONE VIOLET PV19. BWS 8. Synthetic organic. Semi-transparent.

RAW SIENNA See BURNT SIENNA.

RAW UMBER See BURNT UMBER.

RED BOLE Also BOLE. See RED OCHRE. Used as a ground for gold leaf and can be used in gesso. Used to be used in toned oil grounds.

RED EARTH See RED OCHRE.

RED IRON OXIDE PR101 or PR102. See MARS RED or RED OCHRE.

ROSE MADDER Also MADDER LAKE. NR9. BWS 6. Natural organic lake. Transparent.

RED OCHRE Also NATURAL IRON OXIDE, ENGLISH RED, PERSIAN RED, RED EARTH, TERRA DI POZZUOLI, TERRA ROSA. PR102. BWS 8. Earth. Variable opacity. MARS RED is very similar.

SANGUINE Red colour for pencil/pastel made of earths/iron oxides.

SAP GREEN Organic. Not permanent. Should be replaced by a mixture of permanent colours. Check Colour Index Generic Names.

SCARLET LAKE See CARMINE or TOLUIDINE RED.

SCHAEFFER'S ACID PY104. BWS 1–2. Synthetic organic. Transparent.

SCHEELE'S GREEN PG22. Not permanent. Inorganic synthetic. ***Toxic***. Very similar to EMERALD GREEN.

SEPIA Natural organic. Not permanent. Semi-transparent. Should be replaced by a mixture of permanent colours, check Colour Index Generic Names. BURNT UMBER is a good match.

SIENNAS See BURNT SIENNA.

SILEX See SILICA.

SILICA Also SILEX. PW27. Unaffected by light. Mineral. Semi-opaque.***Toxic***. Powdered quartz. Inert pigment. Good tooth for grounds and possible stabilizer for paints.

STRONTIUM SALT PR48:3. BWS 7–8, reduced in tint. Synthetic organic. Transparent.

STRONTIUM YELLOW PY32. BWS 7. Inorganic synthetic. Semi-transparent. ***Toxic***.

SYNTHETIC IRON OXIDES See MARS COLOURS.

TALC Also ASBESTINE, FRENCH CHALK. PW26. Unaffected by light. Mineral. ***Toxic***. Inert pigment. Used in white for pastels.

TARTRAZINE YELLOW PY100. BWS 1–2. Synthetic organic. Transparent.

TERRA DI POZZUOLI See RED OCHRE.

TERRA ROSA See RED OCHRE.

TERRE VERTE See GREEN EARTH.

TETRACHLOROISOINDOLINONE See ISOINDOLINONE YELLOW.

THENARD'S BLUE See COBALT BLUE.

THIOINDIGO PR88. BWS 6–7. In tint BWS 6. Synthetic organic. Semi-opaque.

TITANIUM DIOXIDE See TITANIUM WHITE.

TITANIUM WHITE PW6. BWS 8. Inorganic synthetic. Opaque. Tends to yellow in oil.

TITANIUM YELLOW See NICKEL TITANATE.

TOLUIDINE RED Also HANSA® RED, HANSA® SCARLET, SCARLET LAKE. PR3. BWS 8. In tint BWS 4. Synthetic organic. Variable opacity.

TRANSPARENT BROWN See BURNT GREEN EARTH.

TRANSPARENT OCHRE See MARS YELLOW.

TURKEY UMBER See BURNT UMBER.

TURKISH GREEN See COBALT TURQUOISE.

ULTRAMARINE ASH Poor quality LAPIS LAZULI.

ULTRAMARINE BLUE Also FRENCH ULTRAMARINE. PBL29. BWS 8. Inorganic synthetic. Semi-transparent. Can darken from atmospheric pollution. See also LAPIS LAZULI.

ULTRAMARINE GREEN PG24. BWS 8. Inorganic synthetic. Semi-transparent. Can darken from atmospheric pollution.

ULTRAMARINE PINK See ULTRAMARINE VIOLET.

ULTRAMARINE RED See ULTRAMARINE VIOLET.

ULTRAMARINE VIOLET Also ULTRAMARINE PINK, ULTRAMARINE RED. PV15. BWS 7–8. Inorganic synthetic. Semi-transparent. Can darken from atmospheric pollution.

UMBERS See BURNT UMBER.

VANDYKE BROWN Also CASSEL EARTH, COLOGNE EARTH, NB8. BWS 5–6. Earth. Transparent. Should be replaced by a mixture of permanent colours, can cause oil films to crack.

VEGETABLE BLACK See CARBON BLACK.

VENETIAN RED See MARS RED.

VERMILION PR106. BWS 7–8. Inorganic synthetic. Opaque. ***Toxic***. Can turn black in daylight. Can be replaced by CADMIUM REDS.

VERONA BROWN See BURNT GREEN EARTH.

VERONA GREEN See GREEN EARTH.

VINE BLACK Also BLUE BLACK, CHARCOAL BLACK, GERMAN BLACK, GRAPE BLACK. PBK8. BWS 8. Inorganic. Semi-transparent.

VIRIDIAN Also GUIGNET'S GREEN, HYDRATED CHROMIUM OXIDE. PG18. BWS 7. Inorganic synthetic. Transparent.

WHITE BOLE See CHINA CLAY.

WHITE LEAD See FLAKE WHITE.

WHITING Also CALCIUM CARBONATE, CHALK, PARIS WHITE. PW18. Permanent. Mineral. Inert pigment. Quite absorbent. Most used in gesso, for opacity in gouache, in white for pastels and for buffering paper. GILDERS' WHITING rather than builders' whiting (which is very dirty and sandy) should be used by artists. Muddy in oil. Raw linseed oil and whiting makes putty for windows.

YELLOW EARTH See YELLOW OCHRE.

YELLOW IRON OXIDE PY42 or PY43. See MARS YELLOW and YELLOW OCHRE.

YELLOW OCHRE Also, NATURAL IRON OXIDE, YELLOW EARTH, YELLOW IRON OXIDE. PY43. BWS 8. Earth. Opaque. Best grades are from France. MARS YELLOW is very similar.

ZINC CHROMATE See ZINC YELLOW.

ZINC OXIDE See ZINC WHITE.

ZINC WHITE Also CHINESE WHITE, ZINC OXIDE. PW4. BWS 8. Inorganic synthetic. Semi-opaque.

ZINC YELLOW Also ZINC CHROMATE. PY36. BWS 8. Inorganic synthetic. Semi-transparent. ***Toxic***. Can turn greenish.

PIGMENTS BY NUMBERS

Abbreviated Colour Index Generic Names

Blacks

NBK6	Bitumen
PBK1	Aniline black
PBK6	Carbon black
PBK7	Carbon black
PBK8	Vine black
PBK9	Ivory black
PBK10	Graphite
PBK11	Mars black
PBK14	Manganese black
PBK19	Davy's grey

Blues

NBL1	Indigo
PBL1	Basic dye toner (blue)
PBL15	Phthalocyanine blue
PBL16	Phthalocyanine blue
PBL27	Prussian blue
PBL28	Cobalt blue
PBL29	Ultramarine blue and Lapis lazuli
PBL33	Manganese blue
PBL35	Cerulean blue
PBL36	Cobalt turquoise
PBL60	Anthraquinone blue

Browns

NB8	Vandyke brown
NB11	Bistre
PB6	Mars brown
PB7	Burnt ochre and burnt umber
PB8	Manganese brown
PB23	Azo condensation brown

Greens

PG1	Basic dye toner (green)
PG2	Basic dye toner (green)
PG7	Phthalocyanine green
PG8	Naphthol green
PG10	Nickel azo yellow
PG12	Ferrous nitroso-beta naphthol lake
PG14	Cadmium green
PG15	Chrome green
PG17	Chromium oxide green
PG18	Viridian
PG19	Cobalt green
PG21	Emerald green
PG22	Scheele's green
PG23	Green earth
PG24	Ultramarine green
PG36	Phthalocyanine green
PG50	Light green oxide

Oranges

PO5	Dinitraniline
PO13	Pyrazolone orange
PO20	Cadmium orange
PO21	Chrome orange
PO34	Pyrazolone orange
PO36	Benzimidazolone orange
PO43	Perinone orange
PO62	Benzimidazolone orange
PO66	Isoindolinone orange

Reds

NR4	Carmine
NR9	Rose madder
NR31	Dragon's blood
PR1	Para red
PR2	Naphtol® AS
PR3	Toluidine red
PR4	Chlorinated para red
PR5	Naphtol® AS
PR6	Beta Naphthol
PR7	Naphtol® AS
PR8	Naphtol® AS
PR9	Naphtol® AS
PR12	Naphtol® AS
PR22	Naphtol® AS

PR23	Naphtol® AS
PR48:3	Strontium salt
PR49	Lithol® red
PR52:2	Lithol® red GG
PR53:1	Lake red C
PR57:1	Lithol® rubine
PR81	Basic dye toner (red)
PR82	Basic dye toner (red)
PR83	Alizarin crimson
PR88	Thioindigo
PR90	Basic dye toner (red)
PR101	Mars red
PR102	Red ochre, light red, burnt ochre, burnt sienna, burnt umber
PR104	Molybdate orange
PR106	Vermilion
PR108	Cadmium red
PR112	Naphtol® AS
PR113	Cadmium red
PR122	Quinacridone magenta
PR144	Azo condensation red
PR146	Naphtol® AS
PR147	Naphtol® AS
PR166	Azo condensation red
PR168	Dibromanthone
PR169	Basic dye toner (red)
PR170	Naphtol® AS
PR173	Basic dye toner (red)
PR177	Anthraquinonone red
PR179	Perylene red
PR188	Naphtol® AS
PR190	Perylene red
PR194	Anthraquinone red
PR206	Quinacridone red
PR207	Quinacridone red
PR209	Quinacridone red
PR224	Perylene red

Violets

PV1	Basic dye toner (violet)
PV2	Basic dye toner (violet)
PV3	Basic dye toner (violet)
PV4	PTMA violet
PV5	Alizarin violet
PV14	Cobalt violet
PV15	Ultramarine violet
PV16	Manganese violet
PV19	Quinacridone violet and Quinacridone red
PV23	Dioxazine violet
PV39	PMA violet
PV40	Anthraquinone

Whites

PW1	Flake white
PW3	Lead sulphate
PW4	Zinc white
PW5	Lithophone
PW6	Titanium white
PW11	Antimony white
PW18	Whiting
PW19	China clay
PW20	Mica
PW21	Blanc fixe
PW22	Barium sulphate
PW24	Aluminium hydrate
PW25	Gypsum
PW26	Talc
PW27	Silica

Yellows

NY24	Gamboge
PY1	Hansa® yellow
PY3	Hansa® yellow
PY4	Hansa® yellow
PY5	Hansa® yellow
PY10	Hansa® yellow
PY12	Diarylide yellow
PY13	Diarylide yellow
PY14	Diarylide yellow
PY16	Diarylide yellow
PY17	Diarylide yellow
PY23	Helio Fast yellow 6GL®
PY24	Flavanthrone yellow
PY31	Barium yellow

PY32	Strontium yellow	**PY97**	Hansa® yellow
PY34	Chrome yellow	**PY98**	Hansa® yellow
PY35	Cadmium yellow	**PY100**	Tartrazine yellow
PY36	Zinc yellow	**PY104**	Schaeffer's acid
PY37	Cadmium yellow	**PY109**	Isoindolinone yellow
PY40	Aureolin	**PY110**	Isoindolinone yellow
PY41	Naples yellow	**PY112**	See PY24
PY42	Mars yellow	**PY128**	Azo condensation yellow
PY43	Yellow ochre	**PY137**	Isoindolinone yellow
PY53	Nickel titanate	**PY139**	Isoindolinone yellow
PY73	Hansa® yellow	**PY151**	Benzimidazolone yellow
PY74	Hansa® yellow	**PY154**	Benzimidazolone yellow
PY83	Diarylide yellow	**PY156**	Benzimidazolone yellow

Appendix A
MEDIUM SPECIFIC BRAND DETAILS

Please read the *Preface* for an explanation of the details within these tables.

The brands included in these tables are of products made specifically for artists. There are obviously many other brands of coloured pencils and inks but only the pigmented types or those popular with artists have been included. Very cheap materials are made either for children or for hobbyists and will not fulfil either of the criteria discussed at the beginning of the *Preface*.

Products included in the tables are listed alphabetically by name of manufacturer.

'Ratings on pencils', 'No ratings' etc. in Tables 6, 7, 8, 9 refer to the manufacturer's lightfastness ratings not the Blue Wool Scale.

Where catalogues are mentioned within the tables, it may be found that individual colour charts are published by companies rather than full catalogues.

Table 1: OIL PAINT; OIL/RESIN; ALKYD PAINT

BRAND	OILS	OILS USED FOR WHITES*	NEW BATCHES OF COLOUR MATCHED TO SET STANDARD	STABILIZERS	DRIERS	EXTENDERS
BLOCKX	Refined poppy and linseed	Poppy	No	No	No	Occasionally. Never more than 10% by weight
DALER-ROWNEY Artists' Georgian	Refined linseed and safflower	Sunflower	Yes	Yes	Yes	Yes
LEFRANC & BOURGEOIS †401 range	Refined linseed and others	Soya	Yes	Yes	Yes	To balance colour range
104 range						To reduce pig-ment content
LUKAS Sorte 1	Linseed: cold-pressed, bleached and filtered	Sunflower	Yes	Yes	Yes	To improve pigments
Studio						To reduce pig-ment content

† 401 range not available in UK.

Table 1: OIL PAINT; OIL/RESIN; ALKYD PAINT (*continued*)

BRAND	OILS	OILS USED FOR WHITES*	NEW BATCHES OF COLOUR MATCHED TO SET STANDARD	STABILIZERS	DRIERS	EXTENDERS
MAIMERI Artisti Classico	Linseed, safflower and poppy	Poppy and safflower	Yes	No	Yes	To balance colour range
MAIMERI Brera						To reduce pigment content
OLD HOLLAND	Cold-pressed linseed	Linseed	No	No	No	No
PEBEO	Linseed, poppy and safflower	?	Yes	Yes	Yes	Yes
PELIKAN Mastercolor Water-soluble oil paint	Stand oil, oil varnish and vegetable oil	Poppy	Yes	Yes	Yes	To balance colour range
ROBERSON	Cold-pressed linseed. Poppy for Ultramarine	Poppy	No	No	No	No
SAX	Refined linseed	Linseed	No	Yes	Only to some colours. Amount stated on tube.	No

SENNELIER	Linseed, poppy and safflower	Poppy and safflower	Yes	Yes	Yes	To balance colour range
SPECTRUM Artists'	Refined linseed, poppy and safflower	Poppy	No	Yes	Only to very slow driers	Only to expensive pigments
Tins						To reduce pigment content
STEPHENSON	Refined linseed and safflower	Linseed and safflower	No	Yes	No	No
TALENS Rembrandt	Cold-pressed linseed and safflower	Safflower	Occasionally	Occasionally	To safflower colours	No
Van Gogh Amsterdam						Yes
WINSOR & NEWTON Artists'	Refined linseed and safflower	Safflower	Yes	Yes	Yes	No
Winton						To reduce pigment content
SCHMINCKE Mussini Oil/resin paint	Linseed, sunflower, poppy. 10% damar and mastic resin to 90% oil	Sunflower	Yes	Yes	Yes	To balance colour range
WINSOR & NEWTON Griffin Alkyd paint	Oil modified alkyd resin	Oil modified alkyd resin	Yes	Yes	Yes	No

KEY: [*] Linseed oil paint is used in underpainting. [?] Information not received [–] Not applicable

Table 2: OIL PAINTSTICKS

BRAND	BINDER	STABILIZER	EXTENDER	FLEXIBILITY ADHESION	LIGHTFASTNESS	DIMENSIONS
GRUMBACHER Pre-tested Tubeless oil colour	?	?	?	?	?	25 × 92 mm
MARKAL Paintstiks	Linseed and wax	?	?	?	?	17 × 115 mm
SHIVA	?	?	?	?	?	?

KEY: [?] Information not received [–] Not applicable

Table 3: TEMPERA PAINT

BRAND	BINDER	STABILIZER	EXTENDER
DALER-ROWNEY	Egg and linseed oil	Yes	No
OLD HOLLAND	Egg and oil	No	No
SENNELIER	Egg, gum, and poppyseed oil	Yes	To balance colour range

Table 4: WATERCOLOUR PAINT

BRAND	BINDER	STABILIZER	EXTENDER	RELATIVE AMOUNT OF PLASTICIZER*	
				PAN	TUBES
BLOCKX	Kordofan	No	No	White cap and pan colours have equal amount of plasticizer	Black cap has more
DALER-ROWNEY Artists	Kordofan	Yes	Yes	—	More
DALER-ROWNEY Georgian	Kordofan and dextrin	Yes	Yes	—	More
LEFRANC & BOURGEOIS Linel	Kordofan	No	No	Available in tubes only	—
LUKAS	Kordofan	Tubes only	To improve pigments	—	More
MAIMERI Artisti Studio	Kordofan	No	To balance colour range	—	More
OLD HOLLAND	Kordofan	No	No	Available in tubes only	—
PEBEO Fragonard	Kordofan	Yes	No	Same	Same
SCHMINCKE Horadam	Kordofan and dextrin	Yes	No	Same	Same
SENNELIER	Kordofan	Yes	No	Same	Same
TALENS Rembrandt Talens	Gum acacia	No	To balance colour range	More	—
WINSOR & NEWTON Artists' Cotman	Kordofan and dextrin	Yes	No	More in some colours	Less in some colours

KEY: [–] Not applicable [*] Amount of plasticizer relative within each brand.

Table 5: GOUACHE

BRAND	BINDER	LIGHTFASTNESS COMPARISON TO THE BLUE WOOL SCALE	PROPORTION OF RANGE WHICH IS 7 OR 8 (BWS)
DALER-ROWNEY Designers'	Dextrin Gum arabic for white	Pigment names in catalogue. 4★ = 8 3★ = 7 2★ = 6/5/4	0 out of 60
LASCAUX	Dextrin and synthetic resin. Paint is less soluble because of synthetic resins.	All colours between 6–8	Not given
LEFRANC & BOURGEOIS Linel	Kordofan	Good range. Colour Index Generic Names not given	Not given
LEFRANC & BOURGEOIS Designers' 35GT	Kordofan	Small range. Colour Index Generic Names not given	Not given
MAIMERI Designers'	Kordofan	Colour Index Generic Names in catalogue	Not given
SCHMINCKE Artists'	Gum acacia, dextrin, and synthetic resins	Colour Index Generic Names not given 5★ = 8 4★ = 7 3★ = 6/5	44 out of 60
SENNELIER	Animal glue	Good range. Colour Index Generic Names not given 3★ = 8/7 2★ = 6/5 1★ = 4/3	26 out of 62
TALENS Designers'	Gum acacia and dextrin	Colour Index Generic Names in catalogue 3★ = 8/7 2★ = 7/6 1★ = 6/5 0 = less than 5	46 out of 67
WINSOR & NEWTON Designers'	Gum acacia and dextrin	Colour Index Generic Names in catalogue AA = More than 7 A = 6 or more	13 out of 120

KEY: [?] Information not received [–] Not applicable [BWS] Blue Wool Scale

Table 6: OIL OR WAX PASTELS

BRAND	BINDER	LIGHTFASTNESS COMPARISONS TO THE BLUE WOOL SCALE	DIMENSIONS
CARAN D'ACHE Neocolor I Wax oil	Waxes	Ratings not on crayons or in catalogue 3★ = 8/7 2★ = 6 1★ = 5/4	8.6 × 100 mm
Neopastel			10 × 68 mm
CONTE Oil pastels	Wax and glycerol	Ratings on colour chart. 3★ = ? 2★ = ? 1★ = ?	10 × 70 mm
FILIA Oil pastels	Synthetic waxes	No ratings	9 × 60 mm
SAKURA Cray-pas	Waxes and beef tallow	Ratings not on pastels or in catalogue. All crayons 2 or more.	11 × 71 mm
SENNELIER	Natural wax and liquid wax	Ratings in catalogue 3★ = 8/7 2★ = 6/5 1★ = 4/3	10 × 66 mm 32 × 98 mm
TALENS Panda	Waxes and mineral oils	Ratings in catalogue 3★ = 8/7 2★ = 7/6 1★ = 6/5 0 less than 5	10 × 67 mm

KEY: ? Information not received – Not applicable

Table 7: PIGMENTED COLOURED PENCILS

BRAND	SOLUBILITY	PROPORTION OF PIGMENT IN PENCIL	LIGHT-FASTNESS COMPARISONS TO THE BLUE WOOL SCALE	PROPORTION OF RANGE WHICH IS 7 OR 8 (BWS)
BEROL Karisma	None	Not disclosed	No ratings given. All pencils between 1–5	—
CARAN D'ACHE Supracolour	Water	80%	Ratings not on pencils or in catalogues 3★ = 8/7 2★ = 6 1★ = 5/4	20 out of 80
Prismalo				11 out of 40
Neocolor II				20 out of 84
CONTÉ Couleur d'art	None	5–17%	Ratings on colour chart 3★ = ? 2★ = ? 1★ = ?	? out of 48
Pastel pencil	Partially water-soluble	5–40%		
Aquarelle	Water	5–17%		? out of 24
C W EDDING Mecanorma Color'art	None	Not disclosed	No ratings	Not given
Aquarelle	Water			
FABER-CASTELL Polychromos	Turpentine	Not disclosed	Majority pencils 6–8 but could be 1–5. No ratings on pencils	Not given
Albrecht Dürer	Water			

Table 7: PIGMENTED COLOURED PENCILS (*continued*)

BRAND	SOLUBILITY	PROPORTION OF PIGMENT IN PENCIL	LIGHT-FASTNESS COMPARISONS TO THE BLUE WOOL SCALE	PROPORTION OF RANGE WHICH IS 7 OR 8 (BWS)
H W PEEL LYRA Rembrandt Polycolour	Turpentine	Not disclosed	Ratings not on pencils or in catalogues but on tin 3★ = 8 2★ = 7/6 1★ = 5/4	40 out of 72
Rembrandt Aquarell	Water		No ratings	Not given
REXEL CUMBERLAND Artists'	None	Not disclosed	No ratings	Not given
Watercolour	Water			
Studio	None			
SCHWAN STABILO Stabilotone	Water	40%	Ratings on pencils and in catalogue 5★ = 8 4★ = 7 3★ = 6 2★ = 5/4 1★ = 3	14 out of 55
Softcolour	Turpentine	20%		45 out of 80
Carbothello	Partially water-soluble	65%		45 out of 80

KEY: [?] Information not received [−] Not applicable [BWS] Blue Wool Scale

Table 8: COLOURED INKS, INCLUDING LIQUID ACRYLICS

BRAND	BINDER	WATER-PROOF	PIG-MENTED	LIGHT-FASTNESS COMPARISONS TO THE BLUE WOOL SCALE	PROPORTION OF RANGE WHICH IS 7 OR 8 (BWS)
CONTE Fluidine	Synthetic resin	No	No	No ratings	Not given
DALER-ROWNEY Khandahar	Shellac	Yes	No	No ratings. Not recommended as lightfast in catalogue	Not given
FABER-CASTELL Higgens pigmented	Trade secret	Yes	No	No ratings	Not given
PELIKAN TYPE 'A'	Shellac	Yes	No	No ratings. Not recommended as lightfast in catalogue	Not given
ROTRING ArtistColor Transparent or opaque liquid acrylics	Acrylic resin	Yes	Yes	Ratings not on bottles or in catalogue. All 8, except gold, orange, yellow = 6.	9 out of 12
SCHMINCKE Aerocolour liquid acrylics	Acrylic resin	Yes	Yes	Ratings on bottles and in catalogue 5★ = 8 4★ = 7 3★ = 6/5	21 out of 37
SENNELIER Colorine 111	Acrylic resin and shellac	Yes	No	All colours 8–5. Ratings not on bottles or in catalogue.	Not given

Table 8: COLOURED INKS, INCLUDING LIQUID ACRYICS (continued)

BRAND	BINDER	WATER-PROOF	PIG-MENTED	LIGHT-FASTNESS COMPARISONS TO THE BLUE WOOL SCALE	PROPORTION OF RANGE WHICH IS 7 OR 8 (BWS)
TALENS Ecoline	Gum arabic	No	No	No ratings. Not recommended as lightfast in catalogue	Not given
Graphic Art Colours liquid acrylics	Acrylic resin	Yes	Yes	Ratings on bottles and in catalogue. Colour Index Generic Names on bottles and in catalogue. 3★=8/7 2★=7/6 1★=6/5 0=less than 5	19 out of 24
WINSOR & NEWTON Drawing inks	Shellac	Yes	No	No ratings. Not recommended as lightfast in catalogue	Not given
Brilliant watercolour	Acrylic resin	No	No	No ratings. Not recommended as lightfast in catalogue	Not given
Liquid acrylics	Acrylic resin	Yes	Yes	AA=more than 7 A=6 or more Colour Index Generic Names in catalogue	

KEY: [?] Information not received [–] Not applicable [BWS] Blue Wool Scale

Table 9: CHALK PASTELS

BRAND	BINDER	LIGHT-FASTNESS COMPARISONS TO THE BLUE WOOL SCALE	DIMENSIONS
CARAN D'ACHE Neocolor II	?	Ratings not on pastels or in catalogue. 3★ = 8/7 2★ = 6 1★ = 5/4	8.6 × 100 mm
CONTE Carré	Aluminium silicate	Ratings on colour chart 3★ = 2★ = 1★ =	6 × 70 mm
Soft			8 × 70 mm
FABER-CASTELL Polychromos	Trade secret	Ratings on pastels 3★ = 8/6 2★ = 5/4 1★ = 3/1	7.4 × 83 mm
MAIMERI	Clay	No ratings	10 × 70 mm
ROWNEY Artists' soft	Natural gum	No ratings	8.25 × 63.5mm
Half length broads			11 × 35 mm
Artists' square			8 × 63 mm
SCHMINCKE	Natural gums, methyl cellulose and gelatin	Ratings on pastels and in catalogue 5★ = 8 4★ = 7 3★ = 6/5 2★ = 4 1★ = 3/2	12 × 65 mm

Table 9: CHALK PASTELS (*continued*)

BRAND	BINDER	LIGHT-FASTNESS COMPARISONS TO THE BLUE WOOL SCALE	DIMENSIONS
SWAN STABILO Carbothello	Synthetic resin	Ratings in catalogue 5★ = 8 4★ = 7 3★ = 6 2★ = 5/4 1★ = 3	6 × 8 mm
SENNELIER A l'écu	Natural resin	Ratings and some pigment names in catalogue 3★ = 8/7 2★ = 6/5 1★ = 4/3	10 × 66 mm 32 × 98 mm
TALENS Rembrandt	Trade secret	Ratings and Colour Index Generic Names in catalogue 3★ = 8/7 2★ = 7/6 1★ = 6/5	11 × 72 mm
UNISON	Various	No ratings	13 × 50 mm 20 × 70 mm

KEY: [?] Information not received [–] Not applicable

Appendix B
TOOLS, BRUSHES, THEIR MAINTENANCE, AND FINE ART GLUES

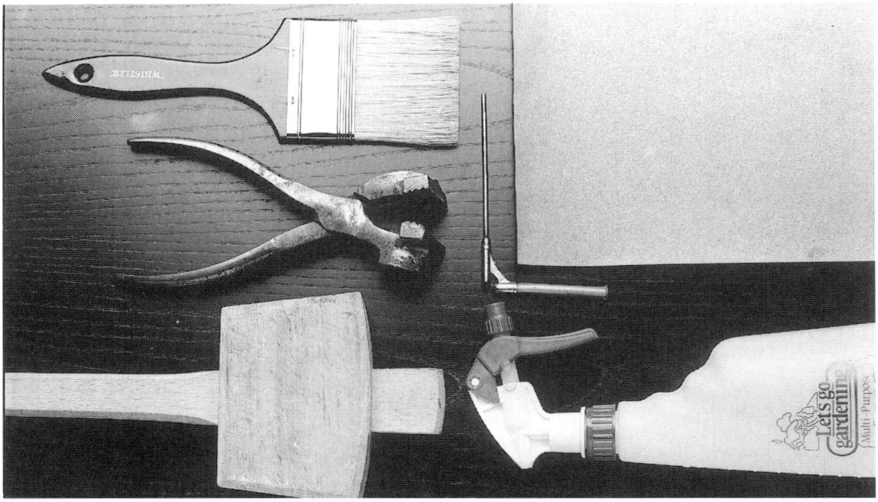

108. Clockwise: *Varnish brush, mouth atomizer, garnet paper, garden spray, wooden mallet, canvas pliers.*

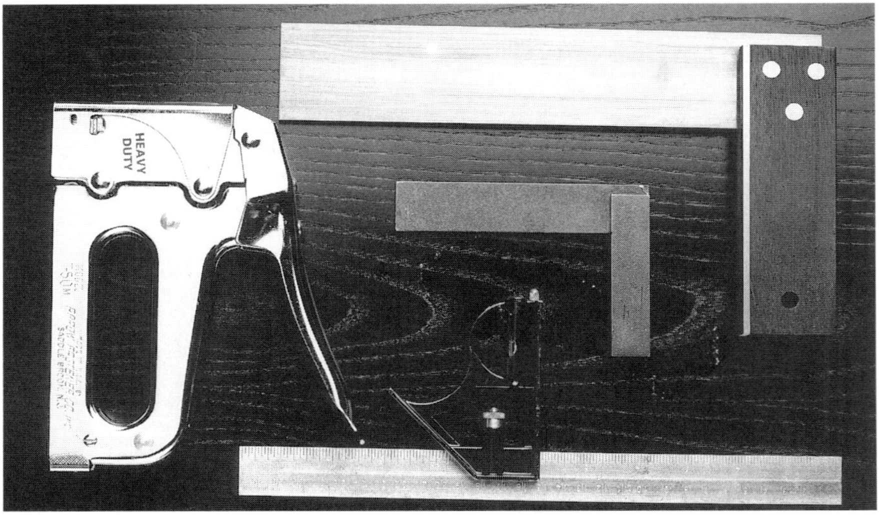

109. Clockwise: *Staple gun, woodworker's try square, engineer's square, combination square.*

TOOLS

Don't be tempted to buy cheap canvas pliers as they will break easily.

BRUSHES FOR ARTISTS

Besides the brushes mentioned within this book there are of course many types of brushes for artists. The more expensive ones will generally last longer, be more responsive or may be made for a specific technique. Use the brushes you like or can afford. See *Bibliography* (page 171) and manufacturers' catalogues for further information.

Cleaning brushes

See also *Health and safety* (page 9) for cleanliness.

N.B. You must avoid skin contact with toxic paints, e.g. white lead, etc. See pigment list (page 131) for toxic pigments. Wear rubber gloves when cleaning brushes, there is no point in rubbing paint into your hands. Do not use a bathroom or kitchen sink, as a residue of paint may be left.

Water-based mediums: Rinse the majority of the paint off in a bowl of water.

Oil-based mediums: Lay an old newspaper out and pour some white spirit on to a page. Wipe the brush up and down on the white spirit until it is completely coloured, then turn the page and repeat. Keep going until there is only a trace of colour coming out and the brush is free of grease; the brush will become grey with the newspaper ink. Dispose of the newspaper safely, it will be very flammable because of the white spirit. Don't put it on an open fire.

Either in a studio sink or a bowl of hot water, wash the brush using soap and warm water. Washing-up liquid can be too harsh for natural hair brushes. Rinse and repeat until the brush is soft and clean. Pour the water from the bowl down the toilet or an outside drain.

Cleaning a muller and plate (slab), or other utensils

As for cleaning brushes except, place the muller and plate on newspaper and use rags or paper towel with water or white spirit to wipe them until there is only a trace of colour left. Wash the muller and plate in warm water and washing-up liquid or soap once or twice until clean. Dispose of the rags or paper towel safely.

RECOMMENDED GLUES FOR FINE ART

PVA (Polyvinylacetate) is recommended. For paper or canvas, use a PVA recommended for paper or craft use; and a PVA wood glue for wood. Acrylic emulsion can be used but is more expensive and is a poorer adhesive.

Use pressure to ensure a good bond. Leave the work to dry between two boards with a weight on top. Use the glue sparingly on paper if it is not stretched, otherwise the paper will cockle. The glue can be thinned with water but it will make unstretched paper cockle more.

A brushed-on, water-based glue, may not be acceptable if you need an absolutely flawless bond with no moisture, e.g. mounting photographs on to supports. Dry mounting or Spray Mount are not recommended because they are acidic and leave brown stains which seep through to the front of the work. Beva 371 film® should be used instead. This is a heat activated film of adhesive which is acid free, transparent, non-yellowing, reversible and can be cut to size with scissors. Its only disadvantage is that it is expensive.

Cut a sheet of glue to size and peel off the white backing. Place the glue film and transparent fronting, glue-side-down on to one of the surfaces to be joined. You can't see the glue, just remember it's between the two backings! Place a sheet of glassine paper on top and using a soft cloth and a hot hairdrier, rub over the fronting, ensuring you have activated the whole film. You can see where the glue has been released from its backing. The fronting can then be peeled off and replaced with the surface which needs to be joined. Using the glassine paper again, gently rub over the picture. Rub over with a soft cloth and the hairdrier to complete the bond. Leave to cool for an hour or so and then check by looking across the support at eye level for any blisters. Be patient and repeat until the bond is perfect. You can try using an iron but take care not to damage your artwork.

Copydex, Cow Gum, Evo-Stik, masking tape and Sellotape are not recommended as fine art glues. They make acidic brown stains on paper which even seep through to the front of the picture. In general, glues for conservation use are much less damaging in artists' work than glues made for hardware use.

Appendix C
CARE OF ARTWORK

STORING WORK

Works of art should be stored in conditions in which you would expect to feel comfortable yourself. Dampness must be avoided to prevent mould growing on paper, canvas, wood or gesso. Extremes of temperature should also be avoided. Work should be kept in the house, not in the garage or attic where temperatures are very cold in the winter and hot in the summer. Extreme cold will cause paintings to crack.

Storing work on paper

Work on paper should be stored between sheets of acid-free tissue in a portfolio. Lay in each piece of work individually. Pack the portfolio evenly, using the whole surface area, so that when shut, it will be packed firm rather than with a bulge in the middle and nothing in the outer edges. The work will get damaged if it moves around inside the portfolio.

If the work is not smudgeproof (charcoal, pastels, etc.) or a thick paint film is likely to be squashed (acrylic or oil) a mount can be used to separate the surface of the picture from the next one. The width of the mount needed will depend on the size of the work. A piece approximately 560 × 760 mm (22 × 30″) will need a mount approximately 38 mm ($1\frac{1}{2}$″) wide to support the piece on top of it. Mounts should be made of acid-free mountcard.

110.
a. *Cross-section of mounts and work sandwich.*

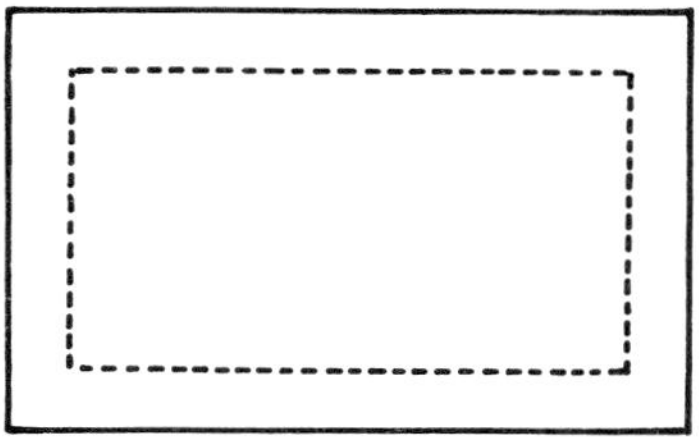

b. *Plan view of work with mount underneath.*

Storing canvases

Canvases should be carefully stacked against an inside wall in the house, i.e. one that is the least likely to get cold or damp. Make sure that all the canvases are leaning against each other's stretchers and not against the canvas.

Storing work on boards

Care must be taken not to drop these boards, as without frames the edges are very susceptible to damage.

FRAMING WORK

Frames for canvases and boards i.e. varnished pictures or encaustic pictures

Frames must be independent structures which the canvases fit into. The painting should not be hung using the stretcher. The stretcher is supposed to be supporting the canvas, not its own weight. The frame should be supporting the stretcher. The frame should not be a very tight fit either, a millimetre or two will allow the wood of the stretcher to expand if it needs to.

Glazed frames

The glass in the frame should not be directly on top of the work. Condensation can build up from lack of circulation and mould will grow on canvas or paper. An oil or acrylic painting will also look squashed if the glass is directly on it. A mount or spacer must be used. A mount is usually coloured and shows as a border within the frame, whilst a spacer fits inside the lip of the frame and cannot be seen when looking at the picture. Both should be acid-free.

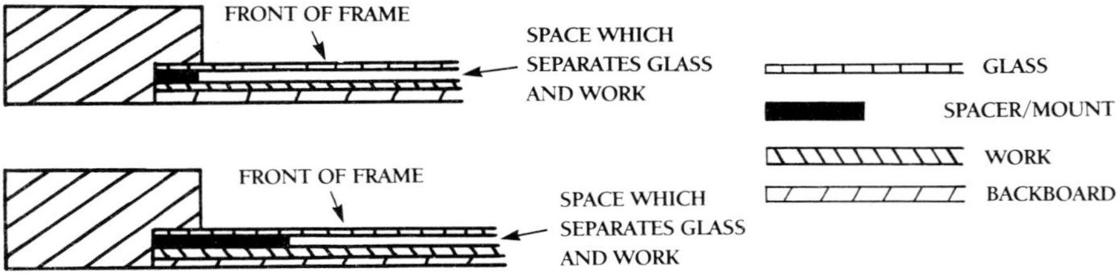

111. *Cross-section of frames showing spacer and mount.*

Backboards

A backing is used to keep dirt out of the frame.

If a canvas already has a paper backing on the back of the stretcher (see page 29) then gumstrip covering the gap between the stretcher and the frame will prevent any dirt getting to the painting. If there is no backing on the stretcher, a backboard must be used to exclude dirt and moderate the effect of changes in moisture from the atmosphere. The backboard does not need to be acid-free. Double stretched canvases will keep the painting cleaner and less susceptible to humidity changes but a backboard will be an added protection.

For work on paper, a hardboard backing is needed. To ensure an acid-free environment, the side of the hardboard which is to be against the paper should be covered in aluminium foil. You can glue it on with PVA glue. Acid-free tissue should be used if any further packing is needed.

Gumstrip should be used to cover the gap between the backboard and the frame to help keep the work dirt-free.

HANGING WORK

Do not hang work over fireplaces or radiators, the heat will dry them out too much.

Bathrooms and kitchens are not recommended either because of the excess of moisture, and kitchen atmospheres are also too greasy.

DAMAGED AND DIRTY WORK

If you really want your work repaired or cleaned without risking further damage, you must take it to a conservator of fine art (see 'Picture cleaners and restorers' in Yellow Pages) and pay for it. To make the right decision and not to damage the work requires a great deal of skill and knowledge. The decision needs to be taken by someone who knows!

See *Bibliography* (page 171) for sources of further but limited information.

GLOSSARY

This glossary includes definitions of terms peculiar to the subject which have not been given within the book. Meanings of words which are not exclusive to the subject can be found in the *Oxford English Dictionary*. The use of at least the Concise edition is recommended.

Where terminology varies between the UK and the USA, a list of equivalent terms is provided at the end of this glossary.

Aluminium stearate: Wax-like material used for stabilizing oil paint.

Binder: The substance which holds the pigment in a paint, ground or drawing material.

Casein: Adhesive made from skimmed milk.

Chassis: Wooden frame, fixed or expandable, used to brace a wood-based board on which to stretch either paper or a canvas. Interchangeable with 'stretcher' and sometimes 'frame'.

Cradled board: Originally a hardwood panel with fixed strips along the grain and movable strips across the grain on the reverse, used to brace the board but still allow it to expand. In this book, 'cradled' is used to mean a wood-based board which has been glued and screwed to a fixed chassis. See fig. 74.

Canvas: Sometimes loosely termed to mean a stretched and primed canvas ready for use or already being painted on.

Double stretched canvas: Two layers of canvas stretched on one frame.

Drying oil: Vegetable oil which dries to a film by oxidization.

Essential oil: Extracted from plants, an oily liquid which is partly volatile.

Fugitive: Indicates instability in the colour of a pigment.

Glazing: Transparent colour over dry underlayer, used to create spatial and/or colour effects. Oil paint offers the widest manipulative possibilities in glazing but any transparent medium can offer glazing too.

Ground: Layer on support which can alter in colour, absorbency or texture. In this book, 'primer' is also used for 'ground'.

Gum: Hardened sap of plants which is either water-soluble or absorbs water.

Handling properties: Group of properties which reflect smoothness, brushability, spreadability, tactility, etc.

Humidifier: Substance or thing which retains moisture or prevents it escaping.

Imprimatura: Coloured veil over a white ground. The term 'veil' is used in this book. See *Coloured grounds* in *Index*.

Industrial methylated spirit: Type of alcohol. Purer than mineralized methylated spirit. Recommended for artists' use where alcohol is required, but is difficult to obtain.

Key: Rough surface.

Livering: Solidification of oil paint within its tube, caused by poor quality pigments or grinding. Nowadays, it is not likely to occur in paint made for artists.

Mahlstick: A long rod with a padded end, used to steady your hand against a painting.

Masking fluid: Rubber latex solution used to mask out areas on paper.

Media: Plural of medium in sense of particular method, e.g. oils, watercolour, etc.

Medium: Used either to indicate a particular method, or to indicate a material used for further manipulation of a method, e.g. glaze medium in oil painting. Plural is mediums.

Mineralized methylated spirit: Type of alcohol. Contains violet dye and more impurities than industrial methylated spirits.
Mineral oil: Type of oil refined from petrol.
Mineral wax: Wax/es refined usually from petrol.
Mull, Mulling: Grind, grinding (rubbing) pigment with muller and plate (slab).
Parchment: Prepared skin of sheep or goat, mainly for calligraphy.
pH of paper: Measure of acidity. pH7 indicates a paper which is acid-free.
Polymerized oil: See *stand oil.*
Primer: Ground.
Proprietary: Patented trade name.
Resin, natural: Hardened sap of plants which is insoluble in water.
Resin, synthetic: Resinous compound, usually synthesized from petrol.
Shellac: Resin secreted by stick insects on certain trees, mainly in India. Available in a number of grades.
Sinking paint: Layer of paint which sinks into underlayer.
Stand oil: In this book stand oil can be assumed to be linseed stand oil. Stand oil is a drying oil which has been processed by heat. It can also be called polymerized oil.
Stretcher: See Chassis.
Support: Material which supports the ground and painting or drawing.
Surfaced: Rough surface.
Tooth: Rough surface.
Toothed: In this book 'toothed' and 'surfaced' are both used to indicate a roughened ground.
Veil: See *imprimatura.*
Vellum: Prepared calf-skin, mainly for calligraphy
Wetting agent: Usually a detergent-based liquid which breaks surface tension of a binder, and 'wets' the pigment or support.

British/American variations in terminology

Chipboard: particleboard.
Hardboard: Masonite.
Paraffin: kerosene.
Sterlingboard: Aspenite.
Wedge (in expandable stretchers): key.

LIST OF SOURCES

This list attempts to include the cheapest or group of cheapest retailers for any similar materials. The more expensive sources are noted after 'Also'. Do check prices – you'll be surprised by the difference.

All brands of paints etc. are listed, as price is not the only consideration. Do look at different ranges of paint; there *are* differences in colours, handling properties etc. which can lead you to prefer one to another. The quality of paints is discussed in the *Preface* (see page 7). Brands are listed in alphabetical order. See *Appendix A* (page 144) for details of individual brands.

Where names of outlets appear more than once, their address is given at the end of the list. Where retail outlets are numerous, the distributors of products are given. They will tell you your nearest retailer. (*D*) denotes 'distributor'. Single retailers will usually sell by post.

Use the Yellow Pages to find local companies, under the headings given.

Local chemists are noted for several items. However, not all pharmacists will be willing to obtain certain items for you – try others. Alternative suppliers/contacts are given where possible for particular items.

Acetone: Local chemist.

Acid-free tissue: See *Paper*.

Acrylic emulsions: Spectrum. Also *Golden* from Direct Art; *Lascaux* from A P Fitzpatrick; Kremer.

Acrylic gesso primer: Made for each brand of acrylic paint. See *Acrylic paint*.

Acrylic paint: *Golden* from Direct Art; *Lascaux* from A P Fitzpatrick; *Liquitex* from Binney & Smith; *Lukas* from Atlantis; *Maimeri* from Osbourne & Butler; *Rembrandt* from Frisk; Rowney, Spectrum, Winsor & Newton. **Water-soluble when dry**: *Lascaux* from A P Fitzpatrick; Quartet, 43 Rookley, Netley Abbey, Southampton SO3 5PH. Phone: 0703 454168.

Acrylic picture varnishes: Check suitability if for oil paintings. Winsor & Newton, Daler-Rowney; *Maimeri* from Osbourne & Butler; *Lefranc & Bourgeois* from ColArt UK; Spectrum.

Acrylic primer: Spectrum. *Roberson* from Cornelissen. Also *Lascaux* from A P Fitzpatrick.

Acrylic size: *Lascaux* from A P Fitzpatrick.

Alkyd grounds: Spectrum. Also oil painting primer from Winsor & Newton; hardboard primer from Daler-Rowney.

Alkyd white: Spectrum, Daler-Rowney, Winsor & Newton.

Aqueous dispersion: Spectrum.

ASTM: American Society for Testing and Materials, 1916 Race Street, Philadelphia PA19103–1187, USA. Phone: 215–299 5400.

Atomizer: Aimer Products, Unit 6, Plaza Business Centre, Stocking Water Lane, Brimsdown, Enfield EN3 7PH. Phone: 081 804 8282. Also local laboratory equipment companies.

Barrier cream: Local safety equipment companies.

Beeswax, natural: Kremer, Atlantis. Also Cornelissen.

Beva 371 film®: Archival Aids, Kremer.

Boards, wood-based: Local timber yards.

Brushes: Check prices at all your nearest suppliers as quality and price varies a lot.

Calcium hydroxide: Local chemist. You may have to buy 400 g (14 oz) of this! Or contact Merck Ltd for help with supplier.

Canvas: Russell & Chapple. Art suppliers' canvas is usually more expensive but you may find different surface qualities. The fine linen (fig. 1) is *Lascaux*'s portrait linen 990; the polyester is *Lascaux*'s P110, both available from A P Fitzpatrick.

Canvas pliers: Atlantis, Cornelissen, Russell & Chapple.

Carnauba wax, natural yellow: Direct Art. Also Cornelissen.

Casein: Cornelissen. Also Kremer.

Casein paints: *Pelikan* from G H Smith.

Chalk pastels: *Conté* from ColArt UK; Daler-Rowney, Faber-Castell; *Maimeri* from Osbourne & Butler; *Schmincke* from Cornelissen; Swan Stabilo; *Sennelier* from H W Peel; *Rembrandt* from Frisk; Unison.

Charcoal, compressed etc: *Conté* from ColArt UK; Faber-Castell.

Chassis, fixed: Local carpenter.

Chinese ink stick and stone: Guanghwa Co. Ltd, 7–9 Newport Place, London WC2 7JR. Phone: 071 437 3737. Also local 'chinese' shops.

Cleaning fluid for spray guns/atomizers: *Schmincke* from Rotring; Winsor & Newton. Use respectively for range used, to ensure proper cleaning. Or seek advice from manufacturer of acrylic emulsion or Langford & Hill. See *Spray guns*.

Cold-pressed linseed oil: Direct Art is much cheaper than others. Also Kremer; Lefranc & Bourgeois, Cornelissen, Winsor & Newton. **Don't** buy hardware shop oils, their quality is probably low.

Colour Index International: The Society of Dyers and Colourists, PO Box 244, Perkin House, 82 Gratton Road, Bradford, West Yorkshire BD1 2JB. Phone: 0274 725138.

Coloured inks: *Conté* from ColArt UK; Faber-Castell; *Pelikan* from G H Smith; Rotring, Rowney; *Schmincke* from Rotring; *Sennelier* contact H W Peel (not held in stock); *Talens* from Frisk; Winsor & Newton.

Colour pastes for acrylic paint: Kremer, Spectrum.

Coloured pencils: Berol, *Caran d'ache* from Jakar; *Conté* from ColArt UK; CW Edding, H V Peel; Faber-Castell, *Rexel*, Swan Stabilo.

Copper plate: Intaglio Printmaker, T N Lawrence.

Damar resin: Cornelissen. Also Stephenson, Kremer, Atlantis.

Damar varnish: Spectrum. Also Stephenson, Direct Art, Cornelissen.

Distilled water: Car accessories shop. Or polite enquiry to laboratories which make and use it!

Double boilers: Local hardware or kitchenware shops. Are very expensive compared to two old pans!

Eggs: Get these as fresh as possible, either from a farm or a busy supermarket.

Empty metal tubes: Cornelissen. Also Stephenson.

Encaustic paints and heated tools: Arts Encaustic, Trem Ar Daf, Glogue, Dyfed SA36 0ED. Phone: 0239 831401.

Fixatives: *Caran d'ache* from Jakar; *Conté* from ColArt, UK; *Lascaux* from Atlantis and A P Fitzpatrick; *Maimeri* from Osbourne & Butler; Rowney; *Sennelier* from Atlantis and H W Peel; *Talens* from Frisk; Winsor & Newton.

Flour paper: Local hardware shop. For large sheets see *Papers* (page 172).
French polish: Local hardware shop.

Garden spray: Local hardware shop.
Garnet paper: Local good hardware shop.
Gelatin: Kremer. Also Direct Art, Cornelissen, Ploton.
Glassine paper: See *Paper*.
Gesso boards: Stephenson, Cornelissen.
Gesso on canvas: Canvex, 9 Bodriggy St, Hayle, Cornwall, TR27 4NB. Phone: 0736 754437.
Gesso powder: Daler-Rowney.
Glass plate (slab), sandblasted, 10 mm ($\frac{3}{8}$") thick: Local glass merchant. Have edges rounded to avoid cutting yourself. Also Cornelissen.
Gilders' whiting: Ploton, Cornelissen.
Glycerine: Local chemist.
Gold wire: Johnson Matthey, local jewellers.
Gouache: *Lascaux* from A P Fitzpatrick; *Lefranc & Bourgeois* from ColArt UK; *Maimeri* from Osbourne & Butler; Rowney; *Schmincke* from Rotring; *Sennelier* contact H W Peel (not held in stock); *Talens* from Frisk; Winsor & Newton.
Graphite, sticks etc.: *Conté* from ColArt UK; Faber-Castell.
Gum kordofan: Kremer, Direct Art. Also Cornelissen.
Gum tragacanth: Kremer. Other suppliers are much more expensive.
Gumstrip: Reeves-Dryad (*D*). Also try local educational suppliers who may or may not have a minimum order or sell to the public. Art suppliers are comparatively expensive.

Hand cleanser, non-petroleum (solvent)-based: *Ultraclean* (pumice based) from T N Lawrence. Also enquire at local safety equipment companies.
Heated tools for encaustic: See *Encaustic paints*. Local hardware shop.

Industrial methylated spirit (IMS): Local chemist should be asked. Some may be prepared to sell you a small amount provided they know what it is for. If it is unobtainable, then ordinary methylated spirits will have to be used.
Inert pigments: See *Pigments*.
Infra-red lamp: Local chemist. Could also make up your own with fittings from lighting shop.

Ketone picture varnishes: Winsor & Newton, Daler-Rowney.

Mason's square: Local good hardware shop.
Metal pen nibs: Philip Poole, widest range.
Metal straight edge (heavy): Local good hardware shop.
Methylated spirits: (mineralized or violet). Local chemist or hardware shop.
Methyl cellulose, *Klucel G*: Archival Aids.
Microcrystalline wax: Alec Tiranti, 27 Warren St, London W1P 5DG. Phone: 071 636 8565. Other suppliers are much more expensive.
Mountcard: See *Paper*.
Muller: Cornelissen. Other suppliers are much more expensive.
Muslin: Russell & Chapple. Also local haberdashery or department store which sells materials.

Nitric acid: Intaglio Printmaker. Also T N Lawrence. You will have to buy 2–2$\frac{1}{2}$ litres (3$\frac{1}{2}$–4$\frac{1}{2}$ pints) of this, unless you know a printmaker who will give you a small amount.

Oil paint: *Blockx* from Green & Stone; Intone; *Lefranc & Bourgeois* from ColArt UK; *Lukas* from Atlantis; *Maimeri* from Osbourne & Butler; *Old Holland* from Atlantis; *Pebeo* from Art Graphique; *Roberson* from Cornelissen; Rowney; *Sax* from A P Fitzpatrick; *Sennelier* from H W Peel; Spectrum, Stephenson; *Talens* from Frisk; Winsor & Newton; *Schmincke Mussini* from Cornelissen; *Griffin alkyd* from Winsor & Newton; *Mastercolor* from G H Smith. Underpainting white from Winsor & Newton. See also *Alkyd white*.

Oil paintsticks: *Markal* from Levermore. *Grumbacher* from M. Grumbacher Inc, 30 Engelhard Drive, Cranbury, NJ 08512, USA. *Shiva* from Shiva Inc, 4320 West 190th Street, Torrance, CA 90509, USA.

Oil (wax) pastels: *Caran d'ache* from Jakar; *Conté* from ColArt UK; *Filia* from Winsor & Newton; *Sakura Cray-pas* from Rowney; *Sennelier* from H W Peel; *Panda* from Frisk.

Orange shellac: Kremer. Other suppliers are far more expensive.

Paint scraper: Local hardware store.

Palette knives: A S Handover. Other suppliers may be more expensive.

Paper, general: *Which Paper?* gives list of suppliers. See *Papers* in *Bibliography*.

Parchment clippings: Ploton, Cornelissen.

Pigments: Kremer has widest choice and is cheapest overall. Also J P Stephenson (small range); Cornelissen. Other art suppliers tend to have very high prices.

Pink-fused alumina: Abrasive Developments Ltd, Norman House, Henley-in-Arden, Solihull, West Midlands B95 5AH. Phone: 0564 792231. A 10 kg (22 lb) handypack is smallest size available, but it will last you a lifetime.

Platinum wire: Johnson Matthey, local jewellers.

Plumbers' solder: Local good hardware shop or plumbing supplier.

Poppy oil: Kremer. Also Spectrum, Cornelissen; *Lefranc & Bourgeois* from ColArt UK. Other suppliers are much more expensive. Don't buy hardware or edible oil, their quality is either lower or of different value.

Proprietary oil with driers: Drying linseed or drying poppy oil from Winsor & Newton.

Protective glasses: Local safety equipment company.

Pumice stone: Local chemist.

PVA glue: Reeves-Dryad (*D*). Also try local educational suppliers who may or may not have a minimum order to sell to the public. Art suppliers tend to be more expensive.

Quills: Philip Poole. Or wild sources.

Rabbit-skin glue granules: Ploton. Also Cornelissen, Rowney, Spectrum, Direct Art, Kremer, Stephenson.

Reed pens: Silk Top Hat Gallery, Quality Square, Ludlow, Shrops. SY8 1AR. Phone: 0584 875363. Philip Poole.

Refined linseed oil: Spectrum. Also Cornelissen, Stephenson, Winsor & Newton. Other suppliers are much more expensive. Don't buy hardware oils, their quality is probably low.

Respirator: Local safety equipment company.

Retouch varnish: Rowney. Also Winsor & Newton; *Lefranc & Bourgeois* from ColArt UK.

Safflower oil: Stephenson. Also Spectrum, Cornelissen. Don't buy edible safflower oil, its quality is of a different value.

Scotch glue: Cornelissen. Also local hardware shop.

Shellac: See **Orange shellac**.

Silicon carbide paper: See *Wet and dry paper*.

Silverpoint, silver and proprietary holder: Cornelissen. Silver from Johnson Matthey, local jewellers.

Sodium benzoate: Local chemist. You may have to buy approximately 400 g (14 oz) of it! Or contact Merck Ltd for help with supplier.

Sodium carboxy methyl cellulose (low viscosity): Direct Art.

Spray guns: Langford & Hill, 38–40 Warwick Street, London W1R 6LS. Phone: 071 437 9945. Check for usage when buying, in case of soluble parts inside the gun.

Spruce boards: Draughtsmen's disused boards can often be found in the studios of old drawing firms. Or Local secondhand office equipment companies.

Stand oil: Direct Art. Also Spectrum, Kremer, Stephenson, Cornelissen. Other suppliers are much more expensive. Don't buy hardware shop oils, their quality is probably low.

Staple gun, Arrow T50: Local hardware shop. This is tough to use but long-lasting and the staples are thick and held by many stockists.

Sterilizing powder: Local chemist.

Stretcher pieces: Bird and Davis, 52 Rochester Place, London NW1. Phone: 071 485 3797. Art suppliers tend to be more expensive. Designs much better in USA. Fixed or expandable stretchers can be custom built by carpenters but will be expensive. D W Stretchers, Unit 118 Faircharm Trading Estate, Creekside, Deptford, SE8. Phone: 081 469 0288.

Sunflower oil: Kremer. Don't buy edible sunflower oil, its quality is of a different value.

Sun-thickened linseed oil: Winsor & Newton. Don't buy hardware store oils, their quality is probably low.

Surgical type gloves: Local safety equipment company.

Tempera: *Old Holland* from Kremer; Rowney; *Sennelier* from H W Peel.

Titanium oil primer: *Roberson* canvas primer from Cornelissen.

Turpentine, artists' quality: Cornelissen, Direct Art, Winsor & Newton. Also Rowney; *Maimeri* from Osbourne & Butler; *Lefranc & Bourgeois* from ColArt UK. Don't buy hardware shop quality turpentine, it will not have had its gummy residue removed entirely.

Underpainting white: See under *Oil paint* and *Alkyd white*.

Varnishing brushes: A S Handover. Other art suppliers likely to be more expensive.

Watercolour: *Blockx* enquire at Green & Stone or Intone, not held in stock; *Lefranc & Bourgeois* from ColArt UK; *Lukas* from Atlantis; *Maimeri* from Osbourne & Butler; *Old Holland* from Atlantis; *Pebeo* from Art Graphique; Rowney; *Schmincke* from Cornelissen and Direct Art; *Sennelier* from H W Peel; *Talens* from Frisk, Winsor & Newton.

Wavy mottler: A S Handover. Other art suppliers likely to be more expensive.

Wax picture varnishes: Winsor & Newton, Rowney; *Lefranc & Bourgeois* from ColArt UK.

Wet and dry paper: Local hardware shop.

White lead primer: Spectrum. Also Kremer. Other brands are far more expensive.

White plastic rubber: Rotring, Staedtler.

White spirit, BS quality: Local hardware shop.

Whiting: See *Gilders' whiting*.

Wooden mallet: Local hardware shop.

(for addresses, see overleaf)

Addresses of Suppliers

Archival Aids, Unit 29, Trent Lane Industrial Estate, Castle Donington, Derby DE7 2NP. Phone: 0332 850450.

Art Graphique, Unit 2, Poulton Close, Dover, Kent CT17 0HL. Phone: 0304 242244.

Atlantis Art Warehouse, Birmingham, Margaret Street, Birmingham B3 3BX. Phone: 021 212 1449.

Atlantis Art Warehouse, Docklands, 2 St Andrews Way, London E3 3PA. Phone: 071 537 2525.

Berol Ltd, (*D*), Oldmeadow Road, King's Lynn, Norfolk PE30 4JR. Phone: 0533 761221.

Binney & Smith, (*D*), Ampthill Road, Bedford MK42 9RS. Phone: 0234 268866.

ColArt UK, Whitefriars Avenue, Harrow, Middlesex, HA3 5RH. Phone: 081 427 4343.

Conté, (*D*): See *ColArt UK*.

L Cornelissen, (*D* and retailer), 105 Great Russell Street, London WC1B 3RY. Phone: 071 636 1045.

Daler-Rowney, (*D*), PO Box 10, Bracknell, Berks RG12 4ST. Phone: 0344 424621.

Direct Art, (*D* and retailer), Winchester School of Art, Park Avenue, Winchester, Hants. SO23 8DL. Phone: 0962 843006.

C W Edding UK Ltd, (*D*), Merlin Centre, Acrewood Way, St Albans, Herts AL4 0JY. Phone: 0727 466 88.

Faber-Castell, (*D*), Crompton Road, Stevenage, Herts SG1 2EE. Phone: 0438 316511.

A P Fitzpatrick, (*D* and retailer), 1 Barnabas Studios, 10–22 Barnabas Road, London E9 5SB. Phone: 081 985 7865.

Frisk Products, (*D*), 3–4 Franthorne Way, Randlesdown Road, London SE6 3BT. Phone: 081 698 3481.

Green & Stone, 259 King's Road, London SW3 5EL. Phone: 071 352 0837.

A S Handover, Angel Yard, Highgate High Street, London N6 5JU. Phone: 081 340 0665.

Intaglio Printmaker, 15 Corsica Street, London N5 1JT. Phone: 071 704 6780.

Intone, 45–47 Newbriggette, Leeds LS2 8JD. Phone: 0532 438370.

Jakar International Ltd, (*D*), Hillside House, 2–6 Frien Park, London N12 9BX. Phone: 081 445 6376.

Johnson Matthey, 43 Hatton Garden, London EC1. Phone: 071 269 8102.

Kremer Pigmente, Farbmühle, D-7974 Aichstetten/Allgäu, Germany. Phone: 07565 1604.

T N Lawrence, 119 Clerkenwell Road, London EC1R 5BY. Phone: 071 242 3534.

Lefranc & Bourgeois, (*D*). See *ColArt UK*.

Levermore & Co., (*D*), 24 Endeavour Way, London SW19 8UH. Phone: 081 946 9882.

Maimeri. See *Osbourne & Butler*.

Merck Ltd, (*D*), (was BDH Ltd) Poole, Dorset BH12 4NN. Phone: 0202 745520.

Osborne & Butler, (*D*), Hartlebury Trading Estate, Hartlebury, Worcs. DY10 4JB. Phone 0299 250 654.

H W Peel, (*D*), Norwester House, Fairway Drive, Greenford, Middlesex. Phone: 081 578 6861.

E Ploton, 273 Archway Road, London N6 5AA. Phone: 081 348 0315.

Philip Poole, 105 Great Russell Street, London WC1B 3RY. Phone: 071 636 1045.

Reeves-Dryad (*D*), PO Box 38, Leicester LE1 9BU. Phone: 0533 510405.

Rexel Ltd, (*D*), Gatehouse Road, Aylesbury, Bucks HP19 3DT. Phone: 0296 81421.

Rotring UK, (*D*), Strathcona Road, Wembley, Middlesex HA9 8QP. Phone: 081 908 2577.

Rowney. See *Daler-Rowney*.

Russell & Chapple, 23 Monmouth Street, London WC2H 9DE. Phone: 071 836 7521.

G H Smith, (*D*), Newcombe Way, Orton Southgate, Peterborough PE2 0UJ. Phone: 0733 370707.

Spectrum Oil Colours, (*D* and retailer). 259 Queens Road, South Wimbledon, London SW19 8NY. Phone: 081 542 4729.

Staedtler (UK) Ltd, (*D*), Pontyclun, Mid Glamorgan CF7 8YJ. Phone: 0443 237421.

J P Stephenson, (*D* and retailer), Walkers Cottage, Drakeholes, Everton, Doncaster DN10 5DF. Phone: 0777 817733.

Swan Stabilo Ltd, (*D*), 74 Buckingham Avenue, Slough, Berks SL1 4PA. Phone: 0753 821941.

Unison Pastels, (*D*), Thorneyburn, Tarset, Northumberland NE48 1NA. Phone: 0660 40457.

Winsor & Newton, (*D*), Whitefriars Avenue, Harrow, Middlesex HA3 5RH. Phone: 081 427 4343.

BIBLIOGRAPHY

Unfortunately, some of these very good books are out of print. Copies can sometimes be found in local or college libraries. The British Library has copies for reference.

Recommended books for further information are listed alphabetically under subject.

American Society for Testing and Materials (ASTM)

Wilcox, Michael. (1991) *The Wilcox Guide to the Finest Watercolour Paints.* W. Australia: Artways.

Brushes

Pearce, Emma. (Nov. 1991) 'Artists' Brushes' in 'Art Materials Directory', *Artists and Illustrators Magazine.*

Smith, Ray. See under 'General m & m'.

Stephenson, Jonathan. See under 'Distemper painting'.

Care of artwork

Smith Ray. See under 'General m & m'.

Casein, gesso, and painting

Mayer, Ralph, See *The Artist's Handbook of Materials and Techniques* under 'General m & m'.

Distemper painting (also size painting)

Kay, Reed. See under 'Tempera ...'

Stephenson, Jonathan. (1989) *The Materials and Techniques of Painting*. London: Thames & Hudson.

Encaustic painting, particularly using oil paint in

Kay, Reed. See under 'Tempera ...'

Stephenson, Jonathan. See under 'Distemper painting'.

Fresco painting

Kay, Reed. See under 'Tempera ...'

Mayer, Ralph. See *The Artist's Handbook of Materials and Techniques* under 'General m & m'.

Smith, Ray. See under 'General m & m'.

General methods and materials (Abbreviation: General m & m)

Ayres, James (1985) *The Artist's Craft.* Oxford: Phaidon.

Bazzi, Maria (1960) *The Artist's Methods and Materials.* London: John Murray.

Bomford, D., Brown, C., Roy, A., Kirby, J., and White, R. (1988) *Art in the Making, Rembrandt.* London: The National Gallery.

Chaet, Bernard (1979) *An Artist's Notebook.* New York: Holt, Rinehart & Winston.

Church, A.H. (1915, fourth edition) *The Chemistry of Paints and Painting*. London: Seeley & Co.

Gettens, Rutherford J. and Stout, George L. (1966) *Painting Materials.* New York: Dover.

Laurie, A. P. (1967) *The Painter's Methods and Materials.* New York: Dover.

Mayer, Ralph. (1991, fifth edition) *The Artist's Handbook of Materials and Techniques*. London: Faber and Faber.
—(1970) *A Dictionary of Art Terms and Techniques*. London: A & C Black.
—(1977, second edition) *The Painter's Craft*, New York: Viking Press, and (1979) New York: Penguin.
Smith, Ray (1987) *The Artist's Handbook*. London: Dorling Kindersley.

Gesso sottile; Gesso, gelatin

Thompson, Jr, Daniel V. (1962) *The Practice of Tempera Painting*. New York: Dover.

Grounds, coloured, toned and dark, effects on oil painting

Smith, Ray. See under 'General m & m'.

Making hardwood panels

Smith, Ray. See under 'General m & m'.

Making watercolours and gouache

Mayer, Ralph. See *The Artist's Handbook of Materials and Techniques* under 'General m & m'.
Stephenson, Jonathan. See under 'Distemper painting'.

Oil media, other ingredients for

Mayer, Ralph. See *Artist's Handbook of Materials and Techniques* under 'General m & m'.

Papers

Turner, Silvie. (1991) *Which Paper?*. London: Estamp.

Pigments

Colour Index International (1987, third ed., third revision) Bradford: Society of Dyers and Colourists (see *Lists of sources*, page 166, for address) and USA: American Association of Textile Chemists and Colorists. Copy in British Library or contact Society of Dyers and Colourists.

Manufacturers' catalogues.

Wilcox, Michael. See under ASTM.

Reference, general

Oxford English Dictionary, Concise edition.

Scraperboard

Mayer, Ralph. See *The Artist's Handbook of Materials and Techniques* under 'General m & m'.
Wehlte, Kurt. (1975) *The Materials and Techniques of Painting*. New York: Von Nostrand.

Silicone ester painting

Mayer, Ralph. See *The Artist's Handbook of Materials and Techniques* under 'General m & m'.

Size painting

See under 'Distemper painting'.

Supports, other, including preparation

See under 'General m & m'.

Sodium carboxy methyl cellulose

Smith, Ray. See under 'General m & m'.

Tempera, further information and recipes

Kay, Reed. (1972) *The Painter's Guide to Studio Methods and Materials*. New York: Doubleday & Co. (First published 1961 as *The Painter's Companion*).

Mayer, Ralph. See *The Artist's Handbook of Materials and Techniques* under 'General m & m'.

Smith, Ray. See under 'General m & m'.

Thompson, Daniel V. See under 'Gesso sottile'.

Toxicity of pigments, solvents

McCann, Michael. (1979) *Artist Beware*. New York: Watson Guptill.

Wilcox, Michael. See under ASTM.

Waxes, other

Mayer, Ralph. See *The Artist's Handbook of Materials and Techniques* under 'General m & m'.

ACKNOWLEDGEMENTS

Thank you to the following to whom I am indebted for helping with technical information although I must take the blame if anything in the book is incorrect: Adrian Abel of Hoechst UK Ltd, Halifax; Jim Patterson of The Two Rivers Paper Company and Roy Perry and the Conservation Department of the Tate Gallery, London.

Thank you to the following who willingly shared their knowledge and experience with me: Douglas Allsop, Judith Chantry, Oola Corneliussen, Joyce Culkin, Richard Day, Terry Jones, Denis Maughan, Mick Miller, Philip Poole, Brian Reynolds and David Stores.

Thank you to the following people and firms for their patient help: Jacques Blockx of Blockx; R J Cross of ICI Colours; Alois Diethelm of Lascaux; Alan Fitzpatrick of A P Fitzpatrick. A R French of Daler-Rowney; Peter Gee of Ciba-Geigy; U Hollmann, H Muller and V J Wengler of Schmincke; Dr Georg Kremer of Kremer Pigments; Peter Longstaff of Abrasive Developments; Ken Medwell of Rotring UK; L Klein Ovink of Royal Talens; Bernard de Roseaux of Lefranc & Bourgeois; R J Rudd of Osbourne & Butler; Dominique Sennelier of Sennelier; P J Staples formerly of Winsor & Newton; and Elizabeth Williams of The Society of Dyers and Colourists.

Thank you to Philip Ryan of Light Matters for the photography.

Thank you to Kevin Grimshaw for the woodwork (figs 72 and 74).

Thank you to Mick Miller for three of the line drawings.

Thank you to Denis Maughan for lending his painting (fig. 43).

Thank you to Kathy Kiely, Mick Miller, Tamsin Newcombe and Christine Pearce for reading the manuscript.

Thank you to Ralph Mayer and Ray Smith whose books have been invaluable.

Thank you to the following for their personal help and support whilst writing this book: A H, Denis Maughan, Sarah Mills, Christine Pearce, Julia Pearce, Richard Pearce, Philip Ryan, V Salmon, Anne Watts and Helen Wire.

Thank you to Bernard Cohen, David Butler, Stephen Farthing, Tess Jaray and Tom Lomax without whose professional support I would not have been able to write this book.

Thank you to the following firms who provided materials for the photographs and drawings: Archival Aids, Buck & Ryan, London; C & A Hardware, Harpenden; L. Cornelissen & Son; Guangwha Co.; Peter McMorine of Henkel Chemicals; Robert Ryan of The Real Artwork Co.; Russell & Chapple; Philip Poole; Poth Hille & Co. Ltd, Two Rivers Paper Company, and Websters (Builders), Harpenden.

Thank you to Nicholas Walt of Cornelissen for his help with the cover photographs.

A final thank you to the endless list of artists, authors, firms and individuals who have also helped.

INDEX

For pigments please see alphabetical list of common names (page 131) and/or the pigment list by Colour Index Generic Names (page 142).

For retail suppliers of materials please see alphabetical *List of Sources* (page 165).